202 Yummy German Vegetarian Recipes

(202 Yummy German Vegetarian Recipes - Volume 1)

Judy Davis

Published on August, 31 2020

Content

202 Awesome German Vegetarian Recipes

***

1. Apple Cream Cheese Kuchen

Serving: 6 servings. | Prep: 40mins | Ready in:

Ingredients

- 1-1/4 teaspoons active dry yeast
- 2 tablespoons warm water (110° to 115°)
- 1 egg
- 1/4 cup warm milk (110° to 115°)
- 2 tablespoons butter, softened
- 2 tablespoons sugar
- 1 teaspoon grated lemon peel
- 1/4 teaspoon salt
- 1-1/4 to 1-1/2 cups all-purpose flour
- TOPPING:
- 4 ounces cream cheese, softened
- 1 tablespoon sugar
- 1 large tart apple, peeled and sliced
- 2 teaspoons butter, melted
- Confectioners' sugar

Direction

- Dissolve yeast in small bowl of warm water. Put 3/4 cup flour, salt, lemon peel, sugar, butter, milk and egg. Whip till smooth. Mix in sufficient leftover flour to make a soft dough, dough will become sticky.
- Transfer to a floured area. With hands dusted with flour, knead for 6 to 8 minutes, till elastic and smooth. Pat the batter into an oiled 8-inch square baking dish. Slightly build up the edges.
- For the topping, mix sugar and cream cheese in small bowl. Slowly distribute on top of dough. Place slices of apple on the surface; brush with the butter. Put on a cover and allow to rise in a warm area till doubled, about an hour.
- Bake for 30 to 40 minutes at 350° or till golden brown and apples are soft. Let cool on the wire rack. Sprinkle confectioners' sugar on top. Chill the remainder.

Nutrition Information

- Calories: 265 calories
- Sodium: 207mg sodium
- Fiber: 1g fiber)
- Total Carbohydrate: 31g carbohydrate (10g sugars
- Cholesterol: 70mg cholesterol
- Protein: 6g protein.
- Total Fat: 13g fat (8g saturated fat)

2. Apple Kuchen

Serving: 12 | Prep: 30mins | Ready in:

Ingredients

- 1 (18.25 ounce) package yellow cake mix
- 1/4 cup margarine, softened
- 1/2 cup flaked coconut
- 4 large Granny Smith apples
- 1/2 cup white sugar
- 1 teaspoon ground cinnamon
- 1 cup sour cream
- 1 egg

Direction

- Preheat the oven to 175 °C or 350 °F. Oil and flour a pan, 9x13-inch in size. Remove skin, core, and slice each apple into eight wedges. Reserve.

- Mix margarine, coconut and cake mix in a medium size bowl till crumbly. Gently press the mixture into prepped pan, building up the edges partially to make a crust. Set wedges of apple over top.
- Combine sugar and cinnamon and scatter on top of cake mixture and apples. Beat the sour cream and egg together in small bowl. Sprinkle on cake surface.
- In the prepped oven, bake for 35 minutes, or till cake edges turn golden and apples are soft.

Nutrition Information

- Calories: 350 calories;
- Total Fat: 14.2
- Sodium: 352
- Total Carbohydrate: 54.4
- Cholesterol: 25
- Protein: 3.4

3. Apple Raisin Crepes

Serving: 1 dozen. | Prep: 20mins | Ready in:

Ingredients

- 1 egg
- 1 cup 2% milk
- 6 tablespoons water
- 1/4 cup canola oil
- 1-1/2 cups all-purpose flour
- 1/4 cup sugar
- FILLING:
- 5 cups thinly sliced peeled tart apples
- 1 cup sugar
- 1/2 cup raisins
- 2 teaspoons ground cinnamon
- 1 tablespoon confectioners' sugar

Direction

- To make batter, mix in a small bowl the oil, water, milk and egg. Mix sugar and flour; stir to egg mixture and blend well. Keep in the refrigerator for 1 hour, covered.
- Mix in a large saucepan the cinnamon, raisins, sugar and apples. Stir and cook for 8-10 minutes over medium heat or until apples are softened; reserve.
- Prepare an 8-inch nonstick skillet that is lightly greased by preheating; place 3 tablespoons of batter into the middle of skillet. Raise and slant the pan to equally coat the bottom. Then cook until top looks dry; flip and cook for 15-20 more seconds. Take to a wire rack. Continue with remaining batter, greasing skillet as necessary. Once cool, pile crepes with paper towels or waxed paper in between.
- Stuff each crepe with 1/4 cup of apples using a slotted spoon; turn up. Cook crepes in a lightly greased large skillet or griddle over medium heat for 3-4 minutes per side or until golden brown. Dust with confectioners' sugar. Serve right away with remaining sauce from apples.

Nutrition Information

- Calories: 488 calories
- Total Fat: 12g fat (2g saturated fat)
- Sodium: 33mg sodium
- Fiber: 3g fiber)
- Total Carbohydrate: 92g carbohydrate (63g sugars
- Cholesterol: 41mg cholesterol
- Protein: 6g protein.

4. Apple Streusel Muffins

Serving: 1 dozen. | Prep: 20mins | Ready in:

Ingredients

- 2 cups all-purpose flour
- 1 cup sugar
- 1 teaspoon baking powder
- 1/2 teaspoon baking soda
- 1/2 teaspoon salt

- 2 large eggs
- 1/2 cup butter, melted
- 1-1/4 teaspoons vanilla extract
- 1-1/2 cups peeled chopped tart apples
- STREUSEL TOPPING:
- 1/3 cup packed brown sugar
- 1 tablespoon all-purpose flour
- 1/8 teaspoon ground cinnamon
- 1 tablespoon cold butter
- GLAZE:
- 3/4 cup confectioners' sugar
- 2 to 3 teaspoons 2% milk
- 1 teaspoon butter, melted
- 1/8 teaspoon vanilla extract
- Dash salt

Direction

- Set oven to preheat at 375°. Use a whisk to mix together the first five ingredients. In a different bowl, whisk together vanilla, melted butter and eggs; add them into the flour mixture, stir till everything is just moistened (batter will stiffen). Fold apples into the mix.
- Fill the batter up to three-fourths full into 12 muffin cups that are greased or lined with paper. To make topping, mix together brown sugar, flour and cinnamon; cut butter into the mix till crumbly. Sprinkle on top of the batter.
- Bake till tested done with a toothpick, for about 15-20 minutes. Cool down in 5 minutes then take out of pan to a wire rack to cool. Mix the ingredients for the glaze; drizzle on the tops.

Nutrition Information

- Calories:
- Total Carbohydrate:
- Cholesterol:
- Protein:
- Total Fat:
- Sodium:
- Fiber:

5. Austrian Apple Twists

Serving: 64 twists. | Prep: 30mins | Ready in:

Ingredients

- 1 package (1/4 ounce) active dry yeast
- 3 cups all-purpose flour
- 1 cup butter, softened
- 3 large egg yolks, beaten
- 1 cup sour cream
- 1/2 cup sugar
- 1/2 cup finely chopped pecans
- 3/4 teaspoon ground cinnamon
- 1 medium tart apple, peeled and finely chopped
- ICING:
- 1 cup confectioners' sugar
- 4 teaspoons whole milk
- 1/4 teaspoon vanilla extract
- Finely chopped pecans

Direction

- Mix together flour and yeast in a big bowl, then put in butter and blend well together. Put in sour cream and egg yolks, mixing well. Form the mixture into 4 balls, then arrange in separate resealable plastic bags or use plastic to wrap them individually. Chill overnight.
- Mix together cinnamon, pecans and sugar, then put aside. Roll each dough ball on a surface coated with flour into a 9-inch circle, then sprinkle apple and sugar mixture on top. Slice each circle into sixteen wedges then roll up, starting from wide edge, and pinch edge to seal. Put on baking sheets coated with grease, point side facing down.
- Bake at 350 degrees until browned slightly, about 16 to 20 minutes. Transfer to wire racks instantly to cool. To make icing, mix together vanilla, milk and sugar until smooth, then drizzle mixture over twists. Use pecans to sprinkle over top.

Nutrition Information

- Calories: 78 calories
- Total Fat: 4g fat (2g saturated fat)
- Sodium: 31mg sodium
- Fiber: 0 fiber)
- Total Carbohydrate: 8g carbohydrate (4g sugars
- Cholesterol: 20mg cholesterol
- Protein: 1g protein.

6. Banana Nut Muesli

Serving: 2 servings | Prep: 10mins | Ready in:

Ingredients

- 1 cup water
- 2/3 cup quick-cooking oats
- 1 firm banana, sliced
- 1/4 cup raisins
- 1/4 cup chopped almonds
- 1/4 teaspoon ground cinnamon

Direction

- Mix all ingredients in a bowl; cover. Refrigerate overnight and serve chilled.

Nutrition Information

- Calories: 307 calories
- Protein: 9g protein.
- Total Fat: 10g fat (1g saturated fat)
- Sodium: 4mg sodium
- Fiber: 7g fiber)
- Total Carbohydrate: 49g carbohydrate (23g sugars
- Cholesterol: 0 cholesterol

7. Basil Brussels Sprouts

Serving: 4-6 servings. | Prep: 5mins | Ready in:

Ingredients

- 2 pounds brussels sprouts, trimmed and halved
- 3 tablespoons water
- 1/4 cup butter, melted
- 1/2 teaspoon salt
- 1/2 teaspoon dried basil
- 1/2 teaspoon pepper

Direction

- In a two-quarts microwavable dish, put in water and Brussels sprouts; cover. Set the microwave on high for 6-8mins until tender-crisp; drain sprouts. Mix pepper, butter, basil, and salt together; toss with the Brussels sprouts until evenly coated.

Nutrition Information

- Calories: 133 calories
- Cholesterol: 20mg cholesterol
- Protein: 5g protein.
- Total Fat: 8g fat (5g saturated fat)
- Sodium: 312mg sodium
- Fiber: 6g fiber)
- Total Carbohydrate: 14g carbohydrate (3g sugars

8. Basil Spaetzle

Serving: 6-8 servings. | Prep: 15mins | Ready in:

Ingredients

- 3 cups all-purpose flour
- 1/3 cup finely chopped fresh basil leaves
- 3 teaspoons salt, divided
- 4 eggs, beaten
- 1/2 cup cold water

- 4 quarts water
- 2 tablespoons butter

Direction

- Combine flour, 1 teaspoon salt and basil in a bowl. Stir in cold water and eggs; mix until the dough is smooth. Boil water and the leftover salt in a large kettle; lower the heat. Press the dough through a colander with a rubber spatula into the simmering water. Simmer for about 2-3 minutes, stirring gently to prevent the spaetzle from sticking together. Strain; toss with butter.

Nutrition Information

- Calories: 233 calories
- Total Fat: 6g fat (3g saturated fat)
- Sodium: 946mg sodium
- Fiber: 1g fiber)
- Total Carbohydrate: 36g carbohydrate (1g sugars
- Cholesterol: 114mg cholesterol
- Protein: 8g protein.

9. Bavarian Noodles

Serving: 5 servings. | Prep: 5mins | Ready in:

Ingredients

- 2 cups uncooked egg noodles
- 1 medium apple, chopped
- 1/4 teaspoon caraway seeds
- 2 tablespoons butter
- 2 tablespoons honey
- 1 tablespoon Dijon mustard

Direction

- Cook noodles following the package directions. In the meantime, sauté caraway and apple in butter in a large skillet until the apple is crisp-tender. Then, stir in the mustard and honey.
- Allow the noodles to drain, then stir into the apple mixture. Finally, cook until heated through.

Nutrition Information

- Calories: 144 calories
- Total Carbohydrate: 22g carbohydrate (10g sugars
- Cholesterol: 27mg cholesterol
- Protein: 2g protein.
- Total Fat: 6g fat (3g saturated fat)
- Sodium: 126mg sodium
- Fiber: 1g fiber)

10. Bishop's Bread

Serving: 1 loaf. | Prep: 15mins | Ready in:

Ingredients

- 1 cup sugar
- 3 eggs
- 1/2 teaspoon almond extract
- 1/2 teaspoon vanilla extract
- 1-1/2 cups all-purpose flour
- 1-1/2 teaspoons baking powder
- 1 teaspoon salt
- 1 cup whole almonds
- 1 cup chopped walnuts
- 1 cup chopped dates
- 1/2 cup each red and green maraschino cherries, drained and halved
- 1 milk chocolate candy bar with almonds (7 ounces), broken into bite-size pieces

Direction

- Beat together extracts, eggs and sugar in a big bowl. Mix together salt, baking powder and flour in a separate bowl, then stir in candy bar, cherries, dates, walnuts and almonds. Stir into egg mixture until combined.

- Transfer into a 9"x5" loaf pan coated with grease and flour. Press dough down firmly to get rid of air spaces, then bake at 300 degrees about 2 hours. Allow to cool about 10 minutes prior to transferring from pan to a wire rack.

Nutrition Information

- Calories:
- Sodium:
- Fiber:
- Total Carbohydrate:
- Cholesterol:
- Protein:
- Total Fat:

11. Black Forest Waffles

Serving: 5 waffles (about 6-3/4 in.). | Prep: 20mins | Ready in:

Ingredients

- 1 cup heavy whipping cream
- 3 tablespoons confectioners' sugar
- 2 ounces unsweetened chocolate, chopped
- 3 tablespoons shortening
- 1-3/4 cups cake flour
- 6 tablespoons sugar
- 1 tablespoon baking powder
- 1/2 teaspoon salt
- 2 eggs, separated
- 1 cup milk
- 1 can (21 ounces) cherry pie filling
- Chocolate sprinkles or fresh mint, optional

Direction

- Beat cream in a small bowl until starts to thickened. Put in confectioners' sugar and beat until hold soft peaks. Chill until ready to serve.
- Melt shortening and chocolate in a microwave, then stir until smooth. Let the mixture cool a bit. Whisk together salt, baking powder, sugar and flour in a big bowl. Whisk milk with egg yolks in another bowl until combined, then stir into the chocolate mixture. Put into the flour mixture and stir just until moistened.
- Beat egg whites in a clean bowl until stiff but not dry, then fold into the batter. In the preheated waffle iron, following the manufacturer's instructions to bake in the preheated waffle iron until set.
- Serve together with whipped cream and pie filling. Put sprinkles on top, if wanted.

Nutrition Information

- Calories: 706 calories
- Protein: 10g protein.
- Total Fat: 32g fat (16g saturated fat)
- Sodium: 567mg sodium
- Fiber: 2g fiber)
- Total Carbohydrate: 96g carbohydrate (52g sugars
- Cholesterol: 157mg cholesterol

12. Blueberry Kuchen

Serving: 12 servings. | Prep: 10mins | Ready in:

Ingredients

- 1-1/2 cups all-purpose flour
- 3/4 cup sugar
- 2 teaspoons baking powder
- 1-1/2 teaspoons grated lemon zest
- 1/2 teaspoon ground nutmeg
- 1/4 teaspoon salt
- 2/3 cup whole milk
- 1/4 cup butter, melted
- 1 large egg, beaten
- 1 teaspoon vanilla extract
- 2 cups fresh or frozen blueberries
- TOPPING:

- 3/4 cup sugar
- 1/2 cup all-purpose flour
- 1/4 cup butter, melted

Direction

- Mix the first 6 ingredients in a bowl. Add vanilla, egg, butter and milk; beat till well blended for 2 minutes.
- Put into a 13x9-in. greased baking dish; sprinkle with blueberries. Mix flour and sugar in a bowl; add butter. Use a fork to toss till crumbly; sprinkle on blueberries. Bake till lightly browned for 40 minutes at 350°.

Nutrition Information

- Calories: 271 calories
- Sodium: 189mg sodium
- Fiber: 1g fiber)
- Total Carbohydrate: 45g carbohydrate (28g sugars
- Cholesterol: 37mg cholesterol
- Protein: 3g protein.
- Total Fat: 9g fat (5g saturated fat)

13. Breadstick Braids

Serving: 4 breadsticks. | Prep: 20mins | Ready in:

Ingredients

- 4 frozen bread dough dinner rolls, thawed
- 2 tablespoons beaten egg
- 1 teaspoon poppy, sesame and/or caraway seeds

Direction

- Slice a dinner roll into 3 pieces, then roll each piece into a 9-inch rope. Put 3 ropes together to braid. Seal by pinching ends and tuck beneath. Do the same with leftover ropes.
- Put on a baking sheet coated with grease, spaced 2 inches apart. Place a cover and allow to rise for 20 minutes, until doubled. Use egg to brush breadsticks, then sprinkle seeds over top.
- Bake at 375 degrees until turn golden brown, about 10 to 14 minutes.

Nutrition Information

- Calories: 109 calories
- Fiber: 1g fiber)
- Total Carbohydrate: 18g carbohydrate (1g sugars
- Cholesterol: 21mg cholesterol
- Protein: 5g protein. Diabetic Exchanges: 1 starch
- Total Fat: 2g fat (0 saturated fat)
- Sodium: 204mg sodium

14. Brussels Sprouts Supreme

Serving: 4-6 servings. | Prep: 15mins | Ready in:

Ingredients

- 1 pound fresh brussels sprouts, trimmed
- 1 cup chopped celery
- 2 tablespoons butter
- 2 tablespoons all-purpose flour
- 1 cup milk
- 1/2 cup process cheese (Velveeta)
- 1/4 teaspoon salt
- Pinch cayenne pepper, optional

Direction

- On every Brussels sprout, slice X at its core. In a big saucepan, insert a small amount of water, celery and the Brussels sprouts. Leave it cooking with a cover on until they become tender and crispy, about 8 to 9 minutes. Insert butter into a big saucepan then start melting it and stirring in the flour until smoothened out. Pour the milk into the pan in a gradual manner. Lead the mixture to boiling point the lower the heat. Continue cooking and stirring until it thickens, about 2 minutes. Insert the salt and cheese, stirring until the cheese melts. If desired, add cayenne as well. After draining the celery and sprouts, finish off by putting the cheese sauce over them.

Nutrition Information

- Calories: 135 calories
- Sodium: 305mg sodium
- Fiber: 3g fiber)
- Total Carbohydrate: 12g carbohydrate (4g sugars
- Cholesterol: 22mg cholesterol
- Protein: 6g protein.
- Total Fat: 8g fat (5g saturated fat)

15. Brussels Sprouts With Green Peppers

Serving: 6 servings. | Prep: 10mins | Ready in:

Ingredients

- 1 pound fresh brussels sprouts, halved
- 1/4 cup chopped green pepper
- 1/4 cup sliced celery
- 1/4 cup chopped onion
- 1 tablespoon butter
- 1/4 teaspoon salt
- 1/8 teaspoon pepper

Direction

- Boil Brussels sprouts in a pot with an inch of water. Lower heat and let it simmer, covered, for 7mins. Meanwhile, sauté onion, celery, and green pepper for 2mins in a big non-stick pan with melted butter. Drain Brussels sprouts and put in the veggie mixture; season with pepper and salt. Cook for 3-5mins while continuously mixing until the Brussels sprouts are tender.

Nutrition Information

- Calories: 82 calories
- Cholesterol: 8mg cholesterol
- Protein: 4g protein. Diabetic Exchanges: 2 vegetable
- Total Fat: 3g fat (2g saturated fat)
- Sodium: 212mg sodium
- Fiber: 5g fiber)
- Total Carbohydrate: 12g carbohydrate (3g sugars

16. Brussels Sprouts With Pecans

Serving: 6 servings. | Prep: 10mins | Ready in:

Ingredients

- 1 pound brussels sprouts, halved
- 1/2 pound pecan halves
- 2 tablespoons butter
- 1/2 teaspoon salt
- 1/4 teaspoon pepper

Direction

- Start by melting butter in a big skillet. Add pecans and Brussels sprouts, sautéing for 5 to 7 minutes until they become tender and crispy. Scatter pepper and salt over the top.

Nutrition Information

- Calories: 128 calories
- Cholesterol: 10mg cholesterol
- Protein: 3g protein. Diabetic Exchanges: 2 fat
- Total Fat: 11g fat (3g saturated fat)
- Sodium: 252mg sodium
- Fiber: 3g fiber)
- Total Carbohydrate: 8g carbohydrate (0 sugars

17. Buttered Poppy Seed Noodles

Serving: 8 servings. | Prep: 5mins | Ready in:

Ingredients

- 1 package (16 ounces) egg noodles
- 1 medium onion, chopped
- 3 tablespoons butter
- 2 green onions, chopped
- 2 tablespoons poppy seeds
- Salt and pepper to taste
- 1 tablespoon minced fresh parsley

Direction

- Following the package instructions, cook the noodles. At the same time, sauté the onion in butter in a large heavy skillet until the onion starts to brown. Let drain the noodles; bring to the skillet. Stir and cook until the noodles start to brown.
- Combine in the pepper, salt, poppy seeds, and green onions; stir and cook for 1 more minute. Use parsley to dust.

Nutrition Information

- Calories: 275 calories
- Protein: 9g protein.
- Total Fat: 8g fat (3g saturated fat)
- Sodium: 44mg sodium
- Fiber: 3g fiber)
- Total Carbohydrate: 43g carbohydrate (3g sugars
- Cholesterol: 59mg cholesterol

18. Buttery Carrots And Brussels Sprouts

Serving: 8 servings. | Prep: 10mins | Ready in:

Ingredients

- 1 pound carrots, cut into 1/4-inch slices
- 3/4 pound brussels sprouts, halved
- 1/4 cup butter, cubed
- 1 tablespoon minced fresh gingerroot
- 1 tablespoon lemon juice
- 2 teaspoons grated lemon zest
- 1 teaspoon sugar
- Salt and pepper to taste
- Minced fresh parsley, optional

Direction

- At moderate heat, boil water in a big saucepan. Add Brussels sprouts and carrots, cooking for 8 to 10 minutes until they tenderize before draining. Put butter into a small saucepan and heat until melted. Insert ginger, cooking for 2 minutes. Insert pepper, salt, sugar, zest and lemon juice. Empty this mixture out atop the vegetables. If desired, add parsley as.

Nutrition Information

- Calories: 96 calories
- Sodium: 88mg sodium
- Fiber: 3g fiber)
- Total Carbohydrate: 10g carbohydrate (5g sugars
- Cholesterol: 15mg cholesterol
- Protein: 2g protein.
- Total Fat: 6g fat (4g saturated fat)

19. Cabbage Tossed Salad

Serving: 12 servings. | Prep: 5mins | Ready in:

Ingredients

- 5 cups chopped lettuce
- 2 cups chopped cabbage
- 2 cups chopped red cabbage
- 2 celery ribs, chopped
- 3 green onions, sliced
- 1/2 cup vinegar

- 1/4 cup vegetable oil
- 4-1/2 teaspoons sugar
- 3/4 teaspoon salt, optional
- 1/4 teaspoon garlic powder
- 1/4 teaspoon pepper

Direction

- In the big bowl, toss onions, celery, cabbage and lettuce. In the small-sized bowl, stir rest of the ingredients together. Add on top of the salad and coat by tossing. Keep chilled for half an hour prior to serving.

Nutrition Information

- Calories: 54 calories
- Sodium: 14mg sodium
- Fiber: 0 fiber)
- Total Carbohydrate: 54g carbohydrate (0 sugars
- Cholesterol: 0 cholesterol
- Protein: 1g protein. Diabetic Exchanges: 1 fat
- Total Fat: 5g fat (0 saturated fat)

20. Caraway Cloverleaf Rolls

Serving: 2 dozen. | Prep: 30mins | Ready in:

Ingredients

- 2 packages (1/4 ounce each) active dry yeast
- 1-1/2 cups warm water (110° to 115°)
- 1 cup whole wheat flour
- 1/2 cup sugar
- 1/2 cup vegetable oil
- 2 teaspoons caraway seeds
- 1-1/2 teaspoons salt
- 3-1/2 to 4 cups all-purpose flour

Direction

- Dissolve yeast in water in a big bowl. Add 2 cups all-purpose flour, salt, caraway, oil, sugar and whole wheat flour, then beat until smoothened. Add enough of the leftover all-purpose flour until a soft dough forms.
- Flip over onto a surface dusted with flour and knead for about 6 to 8 minutes until pliable and smooth. Put in a bowl coated with cooking spray, flipping once to grease the top. Put on a cover and allow to rise for about an hour in a warm area until doubled.
- Punch down the dough. Flip out onto a surface covered with a thin layer of flour. Split in half, then split each half into 36 pieces. Form into balls and put 3 balls each in greased muffin cups. Put on a cover and allow to rise for around 30 minutes until doubled.
- Bake for 15 to 18 minutes at 375 degrees or until golden brown. Take it out of the pans, then transfer to wire racks.

Nutrition Information

- Calories: 141 calories
- Protein: 3g protein.
- Total Fat: 5g fat (1g saturated fat)
- Sodium: 148mg sodium
- Fiber: 1g fiber)
- Total Carbohydrate: 22g carbohydrate (4g sugars
- Cholesterol: 0 cholesterol

21. Caraway Dill Bread

Serving: 1 loaf (1 pound, 16 slices). | Prep: 5mins | Ready in:

Ingredients

- 2/3 cup water (70° to 80°)
- 1 tablespoon butter, softened
- 1 tablespoon nonfat dry milk powder
- 2 tablespoons sugar
- 1 teaspoon salt
- 2 tablespoons dried parsley flakes
- 1 tablespoon caraway seeds
- 1 tablespoon dill weed

- 2 cups bread flour
- 1-1/2 teaspoons active dry yeast

Direction

- Put all the ingredients in the bread machine pan in sequence recommended by the manufacturer. Choose basic bread setting. Select loaf size and crust color if provided.
- Bake following the machine instructions; monitor dough after 5 minutes of mixing, put 1 or 2 tablespoons of flour or water if necessary.

Nutrition Information

- Calories: 67 calories
- Sodium: 158mg sodium
- Fiber: 1g fiber)
- Total Carbohydrate: 13g carbohydrate (2g sugars
- Cholesterol: 2mg cholesterol
- Protein: 2g protein.
- Total Fat: 1g fat (0 saturated fat)

22. Caraway Rolls

Serving: 2 dozen. | Prep: 15mins | Ready in:

Ingredients

- 2 packages (1/4 ounce each) active dry yeast
- 1/2 cup warm water (110° to 115°)
- 2 tablespoons caraway seeds
- 2 cups (16 ounces) 4% cottage cheese
- 1/2 teaspoon baking soda
- 1/4 cup sugar
- 2-1/2 teaspoons salt
- 2 large eggs, beaten
- 4-1/2 to 5 cups all-purpose flour
- 1 tablespoon butter, melted

Direction

- Dissolve the yeast in water in large bowl. Pour in caraway seeds. Heat the cottage cheese in a small saucepan to lukewarm. Pour in baking soda and combine well. Mix into the yeast mixture. Add eggs, salt and sugar and combine well. Slowly mix in enough of flour to make a soft dough. Cover the dough and allow to rise for about 1 hour in a warm place until doubled. Mix down.
- Transfer to a lightly floured surface and then divide into 24 pieces. Transfer into well-greased muffin cups. Cover and allow to rise for about 35 minutes until doubled.
- Bake for 18 to 20 minutes at 350°. Transfer onto wire racks and brush it with melted butter.

Nutrition Information

- Calories: 20 calories
- Protein: 2g protein.
- Total Fat: 1g fat (1g saturated fat)
- Sodium: 67mg sodium
- Fiber: 0 fiber)
- Total Carbohydrate: 1g carbohydrate (1g sugars
- Cholesterol: 4mg cholesterol

23. Caraway Rye Bread

Serving: 20 | Prep: 20mins | Ready in:

Ingredients

- 2 (.25 ounce) packages active dry yeast
- 2 cups warm water (110 degrees to 115 degrees), divided
- 1/4 cup packed brown sugar
- 1 tablespoon caraway seed
- 1 tablespoon vegetable oil
- 2 teaspoons salt
- 2 1/2 cups rye flour
- 2 3/4 cups all-purpose flour, divided

Direction

- In a half cup of warm water, dissolve yeast in a big mixing bowl. Put in salt, caraway, brown sugar, oil and the rest of the water. Stir well. Mix in 1 cup of all-purpose flour and rye flour. Stir until it becomes smooth. Put in enough of the rest of the all-purpose flour to make a soft dough. Transfer into floured surface. Knead for 6-8 minutes until it becomes elastic and smooth. Put in an oiled bowl and flip once to oil the top. Put cover and allow to rise for 1 hour until it doubles in size in a warm spot. Press down dough and cut into half. Form the halves into a ball and put in 2 8in greased round cake pans. Flatten the balls measuring 6in in diameter. Put cover and allow to rise for 30 minutes until just doubled in size. Bake at 190°C (375°F) until it becomes golden brown in color, about 25-30 minutes.

Nutrition Information

24. Caraway Rye Muffins

Serving: 10 muffins. | Prep: 10mins | Ready in:

Ingredients

- 1 cup rye flour
- 3/4 cup all-purpose flour
- 1/4 cup sugar
- 2-1/2 teaspoons baking powder
- 1/2 teaspoon salt
- 1/2 teaspoon caraway seeds
- 3/4 cup shredded cheddar cheese
- 1 egg, beaten
- 3/4 cup milk
- 1/3 cup vegetable oil

Direction

- Mix together caraway seeds, salt, baking powder, sugar and flours in a big bowl, then stir in cheese. Mix together oil, milk and egg, then stir into flour mixture just until blended.
- Fill batter into muffin cups coated with grease or lined with paper until 2/3 full. Bake at 400 degrees until a toothpick exits clean after being inserted in the center, about 20 to 23 minutes. Allow to cool about 5 minutes prior to transferring from pan to a wire rack, then serve warm.

Nutrition Information

- Calories: 203 calories
- Cholesterol: 33mg cholesterol
- Protein: 5g protein.
- Total Fat: 11g fat (3g saturated fat)
- Sodium: 285mg sodium
- Fiber: 2g fiber)
- Total Carbohydrate: 21g carbohydrate (6g sugars

25. Caraway Seed Rye Bread

Serving: 2 loaves. | Prep: 20mins | Ready in:

Ingredients

- 2 packages (1/4 ounce each) active dry yeast
- 2 cups warm water (110° to 115°), divided
- 1/4 cup packed brown sugar
- 1 tablespoon caraway seeds
- 1 tablespoon canola oil
- 2 teaspoons salt
- 2-1/2 cups rye flour
- 2-3/4 to 3-1/4 cups all-purpose flour, divided

Direction

- Dissolve yeast in a big bowl with 1/2 cup of warm water. Put in leftover water, salt, oil, caraway and brown sugar, mixing well. Stir in 1 cup of all-purpose flour and rye flour, beating until smooth. Put in enough amount of all-purpose flour to make a soft dough.

- Turn dough out on a surface coated with flour and knead for 6 to 8 minutes, until elastic and smooth. Put dough into a bowl coated with grease and turn one time to grease top. Place a cover and allow to rise in a warm area for an hour, until doubled.
- Punch dough down and split in 2 even portions. Form each portion into a ball and put in 2 8-inch round baking pans or ovenproof skillets coated with grease. Flatten balls to a circle with diameter of 6 inches. Place a cover and allow to rise for a half hour, until almost doubled. Bake at 375 degrees until turn golden brown, about 25 to 30 minutes.

Nutrition Information

- Calories: 126 calories
- Total Fat: 1g fat (0 saturated fat)
- Sodium: 238mg sodium
- Fiber: 3g fiber)
- Total Carbohydrate: 26g carbohydrate (4g sugars
- Cholesterol: 0 cholesterol
- Protein: 3g protein.

26. Caraway Wheat Biscuits

Serving: about 1 dozen. | Prep: 20mins | Ready in:

Ingredients

- 2-1/2 cups whole wheat flour
- 2 tablespoons caraway seeds
- 1 tablespoon baking powder
- 1/8 teaspoon salt
- 1-1/3 cups grated onions (about 3 medium)
- 2 eggs, beaten
- 1/2 cup vegetable oil

Direction

- Combine salt, baking powder, caraway seeds, and flour in a large bowl. Combine oil, eggs, and onions in the small bowl; mix into dry ingredients just till gets moistened.
- Transfer onto floured surface. Rolling dough till gets 3/4-inch of thickness; flour a 2-inch biscuit cutter and use it for cutting. Put on a greased baking sheet, 1 inch apart. Allow to bake for 10-15 minutes at 425 degrees till golden brown. Serve biscuits warm.

Nutrition Information

- Calories: 188 calories
- Sodium: 137mg sodium
- Fiber: 4g fiber)
- Total Carbohydrate: 20g carbohydrate (2g sugars
- Cholesterol: 35mg cholesterol
- Protein: 5g protein.
- Total Fat: 11g fat (2g saturated fat)

27. Caraway Yeast Bread

Serving: 1 loaf (16 slices). | Prep: 20mins | Ready in:

Ingredients

- 1 package (1/4 ounce) active dry yeast
- 1 cup warm milk (110° to 115°)
- 2 tablespoons honey
- 2 tablespoons butter, softened
- 1 egg, lightly beaten
- 1 tablespoon caraway seeds
- 1-1/2 teaspoons salt
- 1 teaspoon celery seed
- 1 teaspoon rubbed sage
- 1/2 teaspoon ground nutmeg
- 3 to 3-1/2 cups all-purpose flour

Direction

- Dissolve yeast in a big bowl with warm milk. Put in the honey; allow to rest for 5 minutes. Put in 1 cup flour, nutmeg, sage, celery seed, salt, caraway seeds, egg and butter. Beat until

- smooth. To form a soft dough, stir in enough remaining flour.
- Knead onto a floured surface for 6-8 minutes until elastic and smooth. Transfer into a greased bowl, flipping once to grease all the surface. Allow to rise, covered, in a warm place for 1 hour until double in size.
- Punch down the dough. Put it into a 9x5-inch loaf pan coated with cooking spray. Cover, allow to rise until doubled for approximately 40 minutes.
- Bake for 22 to 27 minutes at 375 degrees or until the bread turns golden brown. Let it cool for 10 minutes before transferring from pan to a wire rack.

Nutrition Information

- Calories: 124 calories
- Total Carbohydrate: 21g carbohydrate (3g sugars
- Cholesterol: 19mg cholesterol
- Protein: 4g protein.
- Total Fat: 3g fat (1g saturated fat)
- Sodium: 248mg sodium
- Fiber: 1g fiber)

28. Cheddar Tomato Dumplings

Serving: 4-5 servings. | Prep: 15mins | Ready in:

Ingredients

- 2 tablespoons finely chopped onion
- 1 tablespoon finely chopped green pepper
- 2 tablespoons vegetable oil
- 2 tablespoons all-purpose flour
- 1 can (28 ounces) diced tomatoes, undrained
- 1 tablespoon minced celery leaves
- 1 teaspoon sugar
- 1/2 teaspoon salt
- 1/4 teaspoon pepper
- DUMPLINGS:
- 1 cup all-purpose flour
- 2 teaspoons baking powder
- 1/2 teaspoon salt
- 2 tablespoons shortening
- 1/2 cup shredded cheddar cheese
- 1/2 cup milk

Direction

- Saute green pepper and onion together in a big skillet with oil until soft. Put in flour and stir well. Mix in tomatoes gradually. Put in pepper, salt, sugar and celery leaves, then bring mixture to a boil on moderate heat. Cook and stir the mixture about 2 minutes, then lower heat and simmer with a cover about 5 minutes.
- In the meantime, to make dumplings, in a bowl, mix together salt, baking powder and flour. Slice in shortening until crumbly. Put in cheddar cheese then stir in milk just until blended.
- Drop on simmering tomato sauce with tablespoonfuls of batter, then place a cover and simmer until a toothpick exits clean after being inserted in a dumpling, about 20 minutes. Avoid lifting the cover while simmering.

Nutrition Information

- Calories: 287 calories
- Total Carbohydrate: 32g carbohydrate (8g sugars
- Cholesterol: 15mg cholesterol
- Protein: 7g protein.
- Total Fat: 15g fat (5g saturated fat)
- Sodium: 916mg sodium
- Fiber: 3g fiber)

29. Cheese Snack Bread

Serving: 20-25 servings. | Prep: 15mins | Ready in:

Ingredients

- 1 package (1/4 ounce) active dry yeast
- 1/4 cup warm water (110° to 115°)
- 3/4 cup warm milk (110° to 115°)
- 2 tablespoons shortening
- 1 tablespoon sugar
- 1 tablespoon salt
- 2-1/4 to 2-3/4 cups all-purpose flour
- TOPPING:
- 2 cups shredded process cheese (Velveeta)
- 1 large egg, beaten
- 1/3 cup milk
- 1 teaspoon finely chopped onion
- Caraway seeds or poppy seeds

Direction

- Dissolve yeast in a big bowl with warm water and allow to stand about 5 minutes. Put in 1 1/4 cups of flour, salt, sugar, shortening and warm milk, then beat the mixture until smooth. Stir in enough amount of leftover flour to make a soft dough.
- On a surface coated lightly with flour, turn dough out and knead for 5 minutes, until elastic and smooth. Put in a bowl coated with grease and turn one time to grease top. Place a cover and allow to rise in a warm area for an hour, until doubled.
- Punch dough down and pat into a 15″x10″x1″ baking pan coated with grease. Place a cover and allow to rise in a warm area for a half hour, until doubled. In the meantime, mix together onion, milk, egg and cheese, then spread the mixture over dough. Use poppy seeds or caraway seeds to sprinkle over.
- Bake about 20 minutes at 375 degrees, until turn golden brown. Slice into squares and serve warm.

Nutrition Information

- Calories: 92 calories
- Protein: 4g protein.
- Total Fat: 4g fat (2g saturated fat)
- Sodium: 399mg sodium
- Fiber: 0 fiber)
- Total Carbohydrate: 10g carbohydrate (2g sugars
- Cholesterol: 16mg cholesterol

30. Cheesy Brussels Sprouts

Serving: 4 servings. | Prep: 5mins | Ready in:

Ingredients

- 1 package (16 ounces) frozen brussels sprouts
- 2 tablespoons water
- 2/3 cup condensed cheddar cheese soup, undiluted
- 1 tablespoon milk
- 1/4 cup dry bread crumbs
- 3 tablespoons chopped walnuts
- 2 tablespoons butter, melted
- Dash of pepper

Direction

- Mix water and Brussels sprouts together in a bowl that's safe for the microwave. For 5 to 7 minutes, leave the sprouts microwaving with a cover on until they turn tender and crispy. During the process, stir them one time. After draining, add milk and soup by stirring them in. Mix the pepper, butter, walnuts and bread crumbs together in a small bowl then scatter this mixture atop Brussels sprouts. Put the microwave-safe bowl into the microwave; leave it cooking for 2 to 3 minutes at a high setting without any cover until thoroughly heated.

Nutrition Information

- Calories: 195 calories
- Total Fat: 11g fat (5g saturated fat)
- Sodium: 419mg sodium
- Fiber: 5g fiber)
- Total Carbohydrate: 19g carbohydrate (1g sugars

- Cholesterol: 19mg cholesterol
- Protein: 8g protein.

31. Cherry Chip Muffins

Serving: about 4 dozen. | Prep: 20mins | Ready in:

Ingredients

- 1-1/2 cups all-purpose flour
- 1/2 cup sugar
- 2 teaspoons baking powder
- 1/2 teaspoon salt
- 1 egg
- 1/2 cup milk
- 1/4 cup canola oil
- 1 jar (10 ounces) red maraschino cherries
- 3/4 cup miniature semisweet chocolate chips
- 1/2 cup chopped pecans
- 1 cup confectioners' sugar
- Softened cream cheese, optional

Direction

- Mix salt, baking powder, sugar, and flour together in a big bowl. Combine oil, milk, and egg in a separate bowl; mix into the dry ingredients until just moistened. Strain cherries, saving 2 tablespoons of juice to use for the glaze. (Dispose the leftover juice or save to use later). Cut the cherries; fold the cherries, pecans, and chips into the batter.
- Drop into miniature or heart-shaped muffin cups lined with paper or lightly coated with oil by tablespoonfuls. Bake at 375° until a toothpick will come out clean when you insert it into the middle, or about 10-13 minutes.
- Let them cool for 10 minutes, and then transfer from the pans onto wire racks. To prepare a thin glaze, mix together the saved cherry juice and confectioners' sugar, drizzle over the muffins. Enjoy with cream cheese if you want.

Nutrition Information

- Calories: 74 calories
- Sodium: 44mg sodium
- Fiber: 0 fiber)
- Total Carbohydrate: 12g carbohydrate (8g sugars
- Cholesterol: 5mg cholesterol
- Protein: 1g protein.
- Total Fat: 3g fat (1g saturated fat)

32. Cherry Chocolate Crepes

Serving: 8 servings. | Prep: 15mins | Ready in:

Ingredients

- 1 package (8 ounces) reduced-fat cream cheese, softened
- 1/2 cup reduced-fat sour cream
- 1/2 teaspoon vanilla extract
- 2/3 cup confectioners' sugar
- 8 prepared crepes (9 inches)
- 1 can (20 ounces) reduced-sugar cherry pie filling, warmed
- 1/4 cup chocolate syrup

Direction

- Whisk the vanilla, sour cream and cream cheese in a small bowl until smooth. Beat in confectioners' sugar gradually. Top each crepe with about 3 tablespoons and spread out to within 1/2 in. of edges, roll it up.
- Place in an ungreased 13-in. x 9-in. baking dish. Bake without a cover at 350° until warm or for 5-7 minutes. When serving, place 1/4 cup pie filling over the crepes and drizzle with 1-1/2 teaspoons chocolate syrup.

Nutrition Information

- Calories: 256 calories
- Protein: 6g protein. Diabetic Exchanges: 2-1/2 starch
- Total Fat: 9g fat (6g saturated fat)

- Sodium: 222mg sodium
- Fiber: 1g fiber)
- Total Carbohydrate: 39g carbohydrate (30g sugars
- Cholesterol: 31mg cholesterol

33. Chocolate Cherry Crepes

Serving: 6 servings. | Prep: 20mins | Ready in:

Ingredients

- 1 can (21 ounces) cherry pie filling
- 1 teaspoon almond extract
- 2/3 cup whole milk
- 2 large eggs
- 2 tablespoons butter, melted
- 1/4 cup blanched almonds, ground
- 1/4 cup all-purpose flour
- FILLING:
- 1 cup heavy whipping cream
- 3 ounces semisweet chocolate, melted and cooled
- 1/4 cup slivered almonds, toasted

Direction

- Mix in a small bowl the almond extract and pie filling; keep in the refrigerator, covered, until chilled. To make crepes, place in a blender the flour, almonds, butter, eggs and milk; then cover and blend until smooth.
- Prepare an 8-inch nonstick skillet that is lightly greased by preheating; place about 2 tablespoons of batter into the middle of skillet. Raise and slant the pan to equally coat the bottom. Then cook until top looks dry and bottom is golden brown; flip and cook for 15-20 more seconds. Take to a wire rack. Continue with remaining batter, greasing skillet as necessary. Pile crepes with paper towels or waxed paper in between.
- To make filling, whisk dissolved chocolate and cream in a mixing bowl until forms soft peaks. Place about 2 tablespoons over each crepe; turn up. Put cherry mixture on top and dust with slivered almonds.

Nutrition Information

- Calories: 433 calories
- Protein: 7g protein.
- Total Fat: 28g fat (14g saturated fat)
- Sodium: 108mg sodium
- Fiber: 2g fiber)
- Total Carbohydrate: 39g carbohydrate (29g sugars
- Cholesterol: 139mg cholesterol

34. Chocolate Cherry Cream Crepes

Serving: 8 servings. | Prep: 30mins | Ready in:

Ingredients

- 1-1/4 cups milk
- 3 eggs
- 2 tablespoons butter, melted
- 3/4 cup all-purpose flour
- 1 tablespoon sugar
- 1/4 teaspoon salt
- 1 package (8 ounces) cream cheese, softened
- 1/2 cup confectioners' sugar
- 1 teaspoon vanilla extract
- 1 can (21 ounces) cherry pie filling
- Chocolate fudge ice cream topping and whipped topping

Direction

- Mix butter, milk, and eggs in a huge bowl. In a separate bowl, combine salt, sugar, and flour and mix it into the egg mixture. Cover the bowl and store inside the fridge for 1 hour. Whisk the cream cheese in a small bowl until fluffy for the filling. Mix in vanilla and confectioners' sugar until smooth; put aside.
- Grease an 8-inches nonstick skillet and heat. Drop 2 tbsp. of the batter into the middle of

the skillet. Gently lift and tilt the pan until the bottom is coated evenly. Cook until its top looks dry. Flip it over and cook for 15-20 more seconds.

- Transfer the crepe into a wire rack. Do the same with the remaining batter, greasing the skillet if necessary. Stack the crepes with waxed paper in between. You can cover and freeze 10 crepes for another use for up to 3 months.
- Fill the center of the remaining crepe with the filling and top with 2 tbsp. of pie filling. Fold the crepe's side edges into the center. Drizzle fudge topping over the crepe and style it with whipped topping. Serve.

Nutrition Information

- Calories: 340 calories
- Cholesterol: 124mg cholesterol
- Protein: 7g protein.
- Total Fat: 16g fat (9g saturated fat)
- Sodium: 243mg sodium
- Fiber: 1g fiber)
- Total Carbohydrate: 42g carbohydrate (29g sugars

35. Chocolate Fruit Crepes

Serving: 10 servings. | Prep: 30mins | Ready in:

Ingredients

- 1-1/2 cups buttermilk
- 3 large eggs
- 3 tablespoons butter, melted
- 1 cup all-purpose flour
- 2 tablespoons sugar
- 2 tablespoons baking cocoa
- FILLING:
- 1 can (21 ounces) cherry pie filling
- 1 can (8-1/2 ounces) sliced peaches, drained and chopped
- 1/2 teaspoon ground cinnamon
- 1/8 teaspoon almond extract
- 1/3 cup hot fudge ice cream topping, warmed
- Whipped cream, optional

Direction

- Mix the butter, eggs and buttermilk in a large bowl. Mix the cocoa, sugar and flour; then stir to buttermilk mixture and blend well. Keep in the refrigerator for 1 hour, covered.
- Prepare an 8-inch nonstick skillet that is lightly greased by preheating over medium heat; drop 2 tablespoons batter into the middle of skillet. Tip and rotate pan to equally coat bottom. Cook until top looks dry; flip and cook for 15-20 seconds more. Take to a wire rack. Continue with remaining batter, greasing skillet as necessary. Once cool, pile crepes with paper towels or waxed paper in between. In a microwave-safe bowl, mix the cinnamon, peaches and pie filling. Place in a microwave, without cover, for 3-4 minutes on high or until heated well, mixing once. Add and stir in extract. Scoop 2 tablespoons filling down the middle of each crepe. Fold sides of crepe over filling. Then drizzle with ice cream topping, and decorate with whipped cream, if desired.

Nutrition Information

- Calories: 241 calories
- Sodium: 109mg sodium
- Fiber: 1g fiber)
- Total Carbohydrate: 41g carbohydrate (26g sugars
- Cholesterol: 74mg cholesterol
- Protein: 5g protein.
- Total Fat: 6g fat (3g saturated fat)

36. Chrismat Stollen With Lemon Glaze

Serving: 2 loaves. | Prep: 25mins | Ready in:

Ingredients

- 1-1/2 cups warm whole milk or warm water (110° to 115°)
- 2 packages (1/4 ounce each) active dry yeast
- 6-1/2 to 7-1/2 cups all-purpose flour, divided
- 1-1/2 cups butter, softened
- 3/4 cup sugar
- 3 large eggs
- 3/4 teaspoon salt
- 3/4 teaspoon grated lemon zest
- 1/2 pound raisins
- 1/2 pound chopped blanched almonds
- 1/2 cup chopped candied fruit
- 3 tablespoons butter, melted
- LEMON GLAZE:
- 1-1/4 cups confectioners' sugar
- 1/4 cup lemon juice
- 1 teaspoon vanilla extract

Direction

- Mix yeast and water or milk together then allow to stand about 3 to 5 minutes. Put in 1 cup of flour, mixing well. Place a cover and allow to rest in a warm area about an hour, until foamy and light.
- Cream sugar and butter together in a big bowl, then beat in 1 egg at a time. Put in lemon zest and salt, then stir in yeast mixture as well as enough amount of leftover flour to make a soft dough. Knead for 6 to 8 minutes, until elastic and smooth. Put in a bowl coated with grease then place a cover and allow to rise in a warm area for an hour, until doubled.
- Punch dough down, then knead in fruit, nuts and raisins. Split dough into 2 portions, then roll each into an oval, 15x8-inch in size. Fold each in half lengthways and put on a baking sheet coated with grease. Use melted butter to brush dough, then cover and let loaves rise for 45 minutes, until nearly doubled in bulk.
- Bake about 30 to 40 minutes at 350 degrees, until turn golden brown. Allow to cool on wire racks. Mix entire of glaze ingredients together and brush on tops of cooled loaves.

Nutrition Information

- Calories: 303 calories
- Sodium: 172mg sodium
- Fiber: 2g fiber)
- Total Carbohydrate: 40g carbohydrate (17g sugars
- Cholesterol: 47mg cholesterol
- Protein: 6g protein.
- Total Fat: 14g fat (7g saturated fat)

37. Christmas Bishop's Bread

Serving: 1 loaf (16 slices). | Prep: 15mins | Ready in:

Ingredients

- 2/3 cup butter, softened
- 3/4 cup sugar
- 2 eggs
- 1 teaspoon vanilla extract
- 2-1/2 cups all-purpose flour
- 3 teaspoons baking powder
- 1/2 teaspoon salt
- 1 cup 2% milk
- 1/3 cup semisweet chocolate chips
- 1/3 cup raisins
- 1/3 cup chopped pecans
- 1/3 cup halved red and green candied cherries
- GLAZE:
- 1 cup confectioners' sugar
- 2 tablespoons 2% milk

Direction

- Set the oven to 375 degrees to preheat. Cream sugar and butter together in a big bowl until fluffy and light. Put in 1 egg at a time while beating well between additions, then beat in vanilla.
- In a separate bowl, whisk together salt, baking powder and flour, then put into the creamed mixture together with milk, alternately, while beating well between additions. Fold in cherries, pecans, raisins and chocolate chips.

- Pour into a 9"x5" loaf pan coated with grease and bake until a toothpick exits clean after being inserted in the center, about 65 to 75 minutes. Allow to cool about 10 minutes prior to transferring from pan to a wire rack.
- Combine together glaze ingredients in a small bowl until smooth, then drizzle over warm bread.

Nutrition Information

- Calories: 370 calories
- Sodium: 328mg sodium
- Fiber: 1g fiber)
- Total Carbohydrate: 54g carbohydrate (31g sugars
- Cholesterol: 66mg cholesterol
- Protein: 5g protein.
- Total Fat: 16g fat (8g saturated fat)

38. Christmas Stollen

Serving: 15 | Prep: 30mins | Ready in:

Ingredients

- 1 tablespoon active dry yeast
- 2/3 cup warm milk (110 degrees F/45 degrees C)
- 1 large egg
- 1/3 cup white sugar
- 1/2 tablespoon salt
- 1/3 cup butter, softened
- 2 1/2 cups bread flour
- 1/3 cup currants
- 1/3 cup sultana raisins
- 1/3 cup red candied cherries, quartered
- 2/3 cup diced candied citron
- 6 ounces marzipan
- 1 tablespoon confectioners' sugar
- 1/4 teaspoon ground cinnamon

Direction

- Dissolve yeast in a small bowl with warm milk. Allow to stand for 10 minutes, until creamy.
- Mix together 2 cups of bread flour, butter, salt, white sugar, egg and yeast mixture in a big bowl, beating well. Put in 1/4 cup of leftover flour at a time, while beating well between additions. Once dough comes together, turn out on a surface coated lightly with flour and knead in citrus peel, dried cherries, raisins and currants. Keep on kneading for 8 minutes, until smooth.
- Coat a big bowl lightly with oil and put into bowl with dough, turning to coat dough well with oil. Use a wet cloth to cover the dough and allow to rise in a warm area for an hour, until twice in volume.
- Coat cookie sheet lightly with grease. Deflate dough and turn out on a surface coated lightly with flour. Roll marzipan into a rope and put in the center of dough. Fold dough over to cover marzipan, then pinch seams of dough together to seal. Put the loaf on prepped baking sheet with seam-side facing down. Use a damp cloth to cover and allow to rise for 40 minutes, until twice in volume. In the meantime, set the oven to 175°C or 350°F to preheat.
- In the preheated oven, bake about 10 minutes, then lower heat to 150°C or 300°F. Bake until turn golden brown, about 30-40 minutes longer. Let loaf cool on a wire rack, then use confectioners' sugar and cinnamon to sprinkle over cooled loaf.

Nutrition Information

- Calories: 178 calories;
- Sodium: 306
- Total Carbohydrate: 28.8
- Cholesterol: 24
- Protein: 2.2
- Total Fat: 6.8

39. Cinnamon Coffee Cake

Serving: 12 | Prep: 10mins | Ready in:

Ingredients

- 1 cup brown sugar
- 1 cup white sugar
- 2 1/4 cups all-purpose flour
- 3/4 cup butter, melted
- 1 teaspoon vanilla extract
- 1 teaspoon baking soda
- 1 teaspoon baking powder
- 2 teaspoons ground cinnamon
- 1/2 teaspoon ground ginger
- 1 egg
- 1 cup buttermilk
- 1/4 cup confectioners' sugar

Direction

- Preheat an oven to 190°C (375°F); grease then flour 9x5-in. baking pan lightly.
- Mix flour, white sugar and brown sugar in a big bowl; mix in melted butter till it looks like coarse crumbs. Add vanilla extract; stir in ginger, cinnamon, baking powder and baking soda. Reserve 1/4 cup mixture for topping.
- Beat buttermilk and egg together in a separate bowl, then slowly stir into the flour mixture. Pour batter in the prepared pan and sprinkle it with the reserved topping.
- In preheated oven, bake for 20-30 minutes till inserted toothpick in middle of cake exits clean; top with powdered sugar. Serve.

Nutrition Information

- Calories: 324 calories;
- Sodium: 248
- Total Carbohydrate: 50.4
- Cholesterol: 47
- Protein: 3.8
- Total Fat: 12.3

40. Citrus Carrots And Sprouts

Serving: 6-8 servings. | Prep: 5mins | Ready in:

Ingredients

- 1 pound fresh brussels sprouts, halved
- 1 pound fresh baby carrots
- 1/4 cup butter, melted
- 1 tablespoon grated orange zest
- 1 tablespoon minced fresh parsley
- 1/2 teaspoon salt
- 5 to drops hot pepper sauce

Direction

- In big saucepan, add Brussels sprouts and carrots with a bit of water. Place a cover and cook 20 minutes, until tender. At the same time, mix the rest of the ingredients. Drain and add the butter mixture into vegetables; coat by tossing.

Nutrition Information

- Calories: 95 calories
- Cholesterol: 15mg cholesterol
- Protein: 2g protein.
- Total Fat: 6g fat (4g saturated fat)
- Sodium: 264mg sodium
- Fiber: 3g fiber)
- Total Carbohydrate: 10g carbohydrate (4g sugars

41. Classic Red Cabbage

Serving: 8 servings. | Prep: 20mins | Ready in:

Ingredients

- 1 medium onion, chopped
- 1/4 cup butter, cubed
- 1 medium head red cabbage, chopped (about 8 cups)
- 1 teaspoon salt

- 1/4 teaspoon pepper
- 2 medium tart apples, peeled and chopped
- 1/4 cup water
- 1/2 cup white vinegar
- 1/3 cup packed brown sugar

Direction

- In the big sauce pan, sauté the onion in the butter till softened. Whisk in pepper, salt and cabbage. Lower the heat; keep covered and let simmer for 10 minutes. Whisk in the water and apples; keep covered and let simmer till the apples and cabbage soften, about 45 minutes more.
- Mix the brown sugar and vinegar; whisk to the cabbage mixture. Boil. Lower the heat; let simmer, without cover, till the apples and cabbage become glazed, about 15 minutes.

Nutrition Information

- Calories: 136 calories
- Sodium: 369mg sodium
- Fiber: 3g fiber)
- Total Carbohydrate: 21g carbohydrate (18g sugars
- Cholesterol: 15mg cholesterol
- Protein: 2g protein.
- Total Fat: 6g fat (4g saturated fat)

42. Coffee Klatch Kolaches

Serving: 2 dozen. | Prep: 45mins | Ready in:

Ingredients

- 1 package (1/4 ounce) active dry yeast
- 1/4 cup warm water (110° to 115°)
- 3/4 cup warm 2% milk (110° to 115°)
- 1/3 cup sugar
- 1/3 cup shortening
- 1 teaspoon salt
- 1/8 teaspoon ground nutmeg
- 2 large eggs
- 4 cups all-purpose flour
- 1 can (21 ounces) cherry pie filling
- 3 tablespoons butter, melted
- GLAZE:
- 1 cup confectioners' sugar
- 1 tablespoon butter, melted
- 5 teaspoons 2% milk

Direction

- In a big bowl of warm water, dissolve yeast. Put in 2 cups flour, eggs, nutmeg, salt, shortening, sugar and milk; whisk till smooth. Put in sufficient leftover flour to make a soft dough. Transfer onto a floured area; knead for 6 to 8 minutes till pliable and smooth.
- Put in an oiled bowl, flipping once to oil the surface. Put a cover and allow to rise in a warm area till doubled in size for an hour.
- Punch down dough. Split into 2 parts; form each 1/2 into a dozen rounds. Put onto oiled baking sheets, 3 inches apart. Flatten every round into a 3-inch disk. Put a cover and allow to rise in a warm area till doubled in size for half an hour.
- Create an indention in the middle of every roll; put a heaping tablespoonful of the filling. Bake till golden brown for 10 to 15 minutes at 350°.
- Brush butter on rolls. Transfer from pans onto the wire racks to cool. Mix glaze ingredients; sprinkle over the tops.

Nutrition Information

- Calories: 187 calories
- Fiber: 1g fiber)
- Total Carbohydrate: 31g carbohydrate (14g sugars
- Cholesterol: 23mg cholesterol
- Protein: 3g protein.
- Total Fat: 5g fat (2g saturated fat)
- Sodium: 127mg sodium

43. Colorful Coleslaw

Serving: 4 | Prep: 20mins | Ready in:

Ingredients

- 1/4 head red cabbage, cored and thinly sliced
- 1/4 head green cabbage, cored and thinly sliced
- 1/2 red bell pepper - cored, seeded, and thinly sliced
- 1/2 yellow bell pepper - cored, seeded, and thinly sliced
- 3 tablespoons thinly sliced snap peas
- 1/4 cup thinly sliced Persian cucumber
- 1/4 cup halved cherry tomatoes
- 1 small onion, chopped
- Dressing:
- 3 tablespoons red wine vinegar
- 2 teaspoons Greek yogurt
- 1 teaspoon sesame oil
- 1 teaspoon celery seed
- 1 teaspoon white sugar (optional)
- garlic powder to taste (optional)
- salt and ground pepper to taste

Direction

- In a mixing bowl, combine the red cabbage, green cabbage, snap peas, cherry tomatoes, red bell pepper, yellow bell pepper, onion and cucumber.
- In a small mixing bowl, stir together the yogurt, vinegar, sesame oil, garlic powder, sugar, celery seed, salt and pepper. Blend well until smooth then pour over vegetables. Toss gently to coat evenly. Refrigerate, covered, for at least two hours to allow the flavors to blend. Serve.

Nutrition Information

- Calories: 78 calories;
- Cholesterol: 1
- Protein: 2.7
- Total Fat: 1.8
- Sodium: 71
- Total Carbohydrate: 14.6

44. Colorful Vegetable Saute

Serving: 8-10 servings. | Prep: 10mins | Ready in:

Ingredients

- 2 medium sweet red peppers, julienned
- 2 medium green peppers, julienned
- 2 medium zucchini, julienned
- 4 medium carrots, julienned
- 1 teaspoon olive oil
- 4 cups thinly sliced red cabbage
- 1/4 teaspoon salt
- 1/4 teaspoon pepper
- 4 teaspoons cider vinegar
- 1/4 cup water
- 1 tablespoon sesame seeds, toasted

Direction

- In the big skillet, sauté carrots, zucchini and peppers in the oil for 5 minutes. Put in pepper, salt and cabbage; sauté for 60 seconds more.
- In the small-sized bowl, mix water and vinegar; add on top of vegetables. Cook while stirring till thoroughly heated or for 2 to 3 minutes. Drizzle with the sesame seeds; cook while stirring for 60 seconds more.

Nutrition Information

- Calories: 45 calories
- Protein: 2g protein.
- Total Fat: 1g fat (0 saturated fat)
- Sodium: 77mg sodium
- Fiber: 3g fiber)
- Total Carbohydrate: 9g carbohydrate (5g sugars
- Cholesterol: 0 cholesterol

45. Confetti Potato Pancakes

Serving: 8 servings. | Prep: 15mins | Ready in:

Ingredients

- 2 (1-1/2 pounds) large potatoes
- 2 medium zucchini
- 2 large carrots
- 1/2 cup finely chopped onion, divided
- 2 eggs, lightly beaten
- 1/2 cup all-purpose flour
- 1 to 2 garlic cloves, minced
- 1/2 teaspoon salt
- 1/2 teaspoon dried basil
- 1/4 teaspoon sugar
- 1 tablespoon canola oil

Direction

- Shred carrots, zucchini and potatoes coarsely, then drain and pat dry. Put into a blender or food processor with a half of the shredded vegetable with 1/4 cup of chopped onion, then cover and process until chopped finely. Turn out into a bowl, then put in shredded vegetables, the remaining onion, sugar, basil, salt, garlic, flour and eggs.
- Heat oil in a big nonstick skillet, then drop into skillet with batter by 1/4 cupfuls, flattening to make patties. Fry until patties are golden brown, then turn and cook on the other side.

Nutrition Information

- Calories: 148 calories
- Sodium: 176mg sodium
- Fiber: 3g fiber)
- Total Carbohydrate: 26g carbohydrate (0 sugars
- Cholesterol: 53mg cholesterol
- Protein: 5g protein. Diabetic Exchanges: 1-1/2 starch
- Total Fat: 3g fat (1g saturated fat)

46. Confetti Salad

Serving: 8-10 servings. | Prep: 15mins | Ready in:

Ingredients

- 6 cups torn salad greens
- 1 can (2-1/4 ounces) sliced ripe olives, drained
- 1 small red onion, halved and sliced
- 1/2 cup chopped sweet red pepper
- 1/2 cup chopped sweet yellow pepper
- 1/2 cup shredded red cabbage
- 1 cup shredded part-skim mozzarella cheese
- 1 to 2 cups Italian salad dressing or dressing of your choice

Direction

- Toss together cheese, cabbage, peppers, onion, olives and greens in a bowl, then serve together dressing.

Nutrition Information

- Calories: 77 calories
- Fiber: 2g fiber)
- Total Carbohydrate: 7g carbohydrate (0 sugars
- Cholesterol: 8mg cholesterol
- Protein: 5g protein. Diabetic Exchanges: 1-1/2 vegetable
- Total Fat: 3g fat (2g saturated fat)
- Sodium: 441mg sodium

47. Contest Winning Vegetable Soup With Dumplings

Serving: 10 servings. | Prep: 25mins | Ready in:

Ingredients

- 1-1/2 cups chopped onions
- 4 medium carrots, sliced
- 3 celery ribs, sliced

- 2 tablespoons canola oil
- 3 cups vegetable broth
- 4 medium potatoes, peeled and sliced
- 4 medium tomatoes, chopped
- 2 garlic cloves, minced
- 1/2 teaspoon salt
- 1/2 teaspoon pepper
- 1/4 cup all-purpose flour
- 1/2 cup water
- 1 cup chopped cabbage
- 1 cup frozen peas
- CARROT DUMPLINGS:
- 2-1/4 cups reduced-fat biscuit/baking mix
- 1 cup shredded carrots
- 1 tablespoon minced fresh parsley
- 1 cup cold water
- 10 tablespoons shredded reduced-fat cheddar cheese

Direction

- Cook celery, carrots, and onions in oil until crisp-tender in a Dutch oven, for 6-8 minutes. Stir in the broth, pepper, salt, garlic, tomatoes, and potatoes. Boil, reduce the heat; put a lid on and simmer for about 15-20 minutes, or until the greens are softened.
- Combine water and flour in a small bowl until smooth, and then stir into the vegetable mixture. Next, bring to a boil, cook and stir until thickened, about 2 minutes. Stir in peas and cabbage.
- To make dumplings: Combine parsley, carrots, and the baking mix in a small bowl. Add water and stir until moistened. Release 10 mounds onto the simmering soup. After that, cover and simmer until a toothpick comes out clean from inside a dumpling (don't lift the lid while simmering), about 15 minutes. Finally, decorate with cheese.

Nutrition Information

- Calories: 258 calories
- Protein: 8g protein. Diabetic Exchanges: 2 starch
- Total Fat: 7g fat (2g saturated fat)
- Sodium: 826mg sodium
- Fiber: 5g fiber)
- Total Carbohydrate: 44g carbohydrate (10g sugars
- Cholesterol: 5mg cholesterol

48. Cranberry Kuchen

Serving: 2 kuchens (12 slices each). | Prep: 30mins | Ready in:

Ingredients

- 2 packages (1/4 ounce each) active dry yeast
- 1/4 cup warm water (110° to 115°)
- 1 cup warm milk (110° to 115°)
- 1/4 cup butter, softened
- 1/4 cup sugar
- 1 teaspoon salt
- 1 egg
- 3-1/2 to 4 cups all-purpose flour
- CRANBERRY SAUCE:
- 2 cups water
- 1-1/2 cups sugar
- 4 cups fresh or frozen cranberries
- EGG MIXTURE:
- 8 eggs
- 3/4 cup evaporated milk
- 3/4 cup sugar
- TOPPING:
- 2 cups all-purpose flour
- 2 cups sugar
- 1 cup cold butter

Direction

- Dissolve yeast in warm water in a big bowl. Add 2 cups flour, egg, salt, sugar, butter and milk; beat till smooth. Mix in enough leftover flour to make a soft dough; don't knead. Cover; allow to rise for 1 hour till doubled in a warm place.
- Cranberry sauce: Boil sugar and water in a saucepan. Add cranberries. Lower heat; cover.

- Simmer for 10 minutes. Take off heat; put aside.
- Egg mixture: Beat sugar, evaporated milk and eggs well in a bowl; divide 1/2 egg mixture between 2 13x9-in. greased baking pans. Put aside leftover egg mixture.
- Punch down dough; halve. Pat every portion over the egg mixture in pans. Put cranberry sauce on dough; drizzle with the leftover egg mixture.
- Topping: In a bowl, mix sugar and flour; cut in butter till crumbly. Sprinkle on top.
- Bake till lightly browned for 25-30 minutes at 350°; on wire rack, cool. Serve warm.

Nutrition Information

- Calories: 387 calories
- Fiber: 2g fiber)
- Total Carbohydrate: 63g carbohydrate (40g sugars
- Cholesterol: 109mg cholesterol
- Protein: 7g protein.
- Total Fat: 13g fat (7g saturated fat)
- Sodium: 232mg sodium

49. Creamy Sprouts N Noodles

Serving: 6-8 servings. | Prep: 20mins | Ready in:

Ingredients

- 1 pound fresh brussels sprouts, quartered
- 2 medium onions, finely chopped
- 4 tablespoons butter, divided
- 1 cup sour cream
- 1 cup 4% cottage cheese
- 1 garlic clove, minced
- 1 teaspoon paprika
- 1/2 teaspoon salt
- 1/4 to 1/2 teaspoon caraway seeds
- 3 cups medium egg noodles, cooked and drained
- 1 cup soft bread crumbs

Direction

- In a saucepan, pour in a small amount of water and the Brussels sprouts; cover. Cook until the sprouts are tender.
- Melt 2tbsp butter in a big pan; sauté onions until golden brown. Take off heat. Mix in caraway, sour cream, salt, cottage cheese, paprika, and garlic.
- Drain Brussels sprouts. Put in the onion mixture along with the noodles. Spread in an oiled and shallow two-quart baking pan.
- Melt left butter and mix with bread crumbs; spread mixture over the casseroles. Bake for 20-25mins in a 375 degrees F oven without cover until golden brown.

Nutrition Information

- Calories: 250 calories
- Cholesterol: 55mg cholesterol
- Protein: 9g protein.
- Total Fat: 13g fat (8g saturated fat)
- Sodium: 369mg sodium
- Fiber: 4g fiber)
- Total Carbohydrate: 24g carbohydrate (6g sugars

50. Crisp Caraway Twists

Serving: about 1-1/2 dozen. | Prep: 15mins | Ready in:

Ingredients

- 1 egg
- 1 tablespoon water
- 1 teaspoon country-style Dijon mustard
- 3/4 cup shredded Swiss cheese
- 1/4 cup finely chopped onion
- 2 teaspoons minced fresh parsley
- 1-1/2 teaspoons caraway seeds
- 1/4 teaspoon garlic salt
- 1 sheet frozen puff pastry, thawed

Direction

- Beat water, mustard and egg together in a small bowl then set aside. Combine onion, cheese, caraway seeds, garlic salt and parsley in another bowl.
- Roll out pastry sheet and brush it with egg mixture. On a lengthwise motion, spread cheese mixture over half of the pastry. Fold pastry over filling and press the edges to seal. Use the rest of the egg mixture to brush the top. Slice crosswise into 1/2 inch strips then twist each strip many times.
- On greased baking sheets, arrange the strips 1 in. apart, pressing the ends down. Bake for 15 to 20 minutes at 350°F or until golden brown. Serve while still warm.

Nutrition Information

- Calories: 179 calories
- Sodium: 185mg sodium
- Fiber: 2g fiber)
- Total Carbohydrate: 16g carbohydrate (1g sugars
- Cholesterol: 32mg cholesterol
- Protein: 5g protein.
- Total Fat: 10g fat (3g saturated fat)

51. Crispy Potato Pancakes

Serving: 6 | Prep: 20mins | Ready in:

Ingredients

- 2 pounds potatoes, peeled and coarsely shredded
- 2 onions, minced
- 3 eggs, beaten
- 1/4 cup all-purpose flour
- 1 tablespoon baking powder
- 1 teaspoon lemon juice
- 1 pinch ground nutmeg, or to taste
- salt and ground black pepper to taste
- 1/4 cup vegetable oil

Direction

- In big bowl, stir lemon juice, baking powder, flour, eggs, onions and potatoes; add black pepper, salt and nutmeg to season. Form the mixture of potato into a dozen equally-sized patties.
- In big skillet, heat the vegetable oil over moderate heat. Working in batches, pan-fry the patties of potato for 7 to 10 minutes till soft and browned on each side. Remove browned patties onto a baking sheet lined with paper towel. Redo with the rest of the patties.

Nutrition Information

- Calories: 268 calories;
- Protein: 7.2
- Total Fat: 11.9
- Sodium: 214
- Total Carbohydrate: 34.6
- Cholesterol: 93

52. Crumb Coated Spaetzle

Serving: 6 servings. | Prep: 15mins | Ready in:

Ingredients

- 2 cups all-purpose flour
- 1 teaspoon salt
- 2 eggs, lightly beaten
- 3/4 cup 2% milk
- 1/2 cup dry bread crumbs
- 1/2 cup butter, melted

Direction

- Mix salt with flour in a small bowl. Mix in milk and eggs until smooth.
- In a big stockpot, add water to fill 3/4 and boil. Press the dough through a colander into the boiling water with a rubber spatula. Gently

stir and cook until the spaetzle is soft and rise onto the surface, or for 4-5 minutes.

- Mix butter with bread crumbs. Remove the spaetzle into a big bowl using a slotted spoon, put in the crumb mixture and stir to coat.

Nutrition Information

- Calories: 363 calories
- Total Carbohydrate: 40g carbohydrate (3g sugars
- Cholesterol: 114mg cholesterol
- Protein: 9g protein.
- Total Fat: 19g fat (11g saturated fat)
- Sodium: 603mg sodium
- Fiber: 2g fiber)

53. Crumb Topped Brussels Sprouts

Serving: 4-6 servings. | Prep: 15mins | Ready in:

Ingredients

- 1-1/2 pounds fresh or frozen brussels sprouts
- 3 tablespoons butter, melted, divided
- 1/4 cup Italian-seasoned dry bread crumbs
- 2 tablespoons grated Parmesan cheese

Direction

- After trimming the Brussels sprouts, slice 'X' into the core of every one. Insert the sprouts into a big saucepan with half an inch of water in it then lead it to boiling point. Lower the heat and leave it simmering with a cover on for 8 to 10 minutes or until they become tender and crispy before draining. Put into a shallow baking dish (1-1/2 quart) that hasn't been greased. Add 2 tablespoons of butter in drizzling motion. Mix the rest of the butter, cheese and breadcrumbs together then empty this out atop the Brussels sprouts. Bake them with a cover on at 325°F for 10 minutes. Remove the cover and continue baking for another 10 minutes.

Nutrition Information

- Calories: 125 calories
- Protein: 5g protein.
- Total Fat: 7g fat (4g saturated fat)
- Sodium: 189mg sodium
- Fiber: 4g fiber)
- Total Carbohydrate: 14g carbohydrate (3g sugars
- Cholesterol: 17mg cholesterol

54. Crunchy Kraut Salad

Serving: 2-3 servings. | Prep: 15mins | Ready in:

Ingredients

- 1 can (14 ounces) sauerkraut, rinsed and well drained
- 1/2 cup chopped celery
- 1/2 cup chopped green pepper
- 1/4 cup chopped onion
- 1/2 cup sugar
- 1/4 cup white vinegar
- 1/2 teaspoon celery seed

Direction

- Mix together onion, green pepper, celery and sauerkraut in a big serving bowl then set aside. Bring vinegar and sugar in a small saucepan to a boil then cook and stir until sugar has dissolved, about 1 minute. Take away from heat and let it cool a little bit. Drizzle over sauerkraut mixture and sprinkle with celery seed. Toss to coat and chill for minimum of 1 hour. Serve together with a slotted spoon.

Nutrition Information

- Calories: 170 calories
- Fiber: 4g fiber)

- Total Carbohydrate: 43g carbohydrate (35g sugars
- Cholesterol: 0 cholesterol
- Protein: 2g protein.
- Total Fat: 0 fat (0 saturated fat)
- Sodium: 894mg sodium

55. Daylily Salad

Serving: 4-6 servings. | Prep: 10mins | Ready in:

Ingredients

- 2 cups daylily buds (about 50 buds), sliced
- 1 cup torn lettuce
- 1/2 medium cucumber, sliced
- 1 medium tomato, diced
- 2 celery ribs, sliced
- 1/4 cup shredded red cabbage
- 3 radishes, sliced
- Salad dressing of your choice

Direction

- Combine radishes, cabbage, celery, tomato, cucumber, lettuce and daylily buds in a large salad bowl. Prepare dressing to serve with.

Nutrition Information

- Calories: 16 calories
- Sodium: 17mg sodium
- Fiber: 1g fiber)
- Total Carbohydrate: 3g carbohydrate (2g sugars
- Cholesterol: 0 cholesterol
- Protein: 1g protein.
- Total Fat: 0 fat (0 saturated fat)

56. Dijon Spinach Salad

Serving: 10 servings. | Prep: 20mins | Ready in:

Ingredients

- 8 cups fresh baby spinach
- 1 cup shredded red cabbage
- 1 cup fresh cauliflowerets, thinly sliced
- 1 cup thinly sliced red onion
- 1/2 cup sliced radishes
- 1/4 to 1/2 cup vegetable oil
- 1/4 cup red wine vinegar
- 2 tablespoons Dijon mustard
- 2 teaspoons sugar
- 1/4 teaspoon salt
- 2 tablespoons sesame seeds, toasted

Direction

- Mix the first 5 ingredients together in a big bowl. Mix salt, sugar, mustard, vinegar and oil in a jar with a tight-fitting lid and shake well. Drizzle the dressing over salad and toss to coat well. Sprinkle on top of the salad with sesame seeds, then serve promptly.

Nutrition Information

- Calories: 80 calories
- Protein: 2g protein. Diabetic Exchanges: 1 vegetable
- Total Fat: 7g fat (0 saturated fat)
- Sodium: 156mg sodium
- Fiber: 2g fiber)
- Total Carbohydrate: 5g carbohydrate (0 sugars
- Cholesterol: 0 cholesterol

57. Dijon Dill Brussels Sprouts

Serving: 4-6 servings. | Prep: 5mins | Ready in:

Ingredients

- 1-1/2 pounds fresh brussels sprouts, halved
- 3 tablespoons butter, melted
- 2 teaspoons Dijon mustard
- 2 teaspoons lemon juice
- 1 teaspoon dill weed

- 1/4 to 1/2 teaspoon salt
- 1/8 teaspoon pepper
- 1 can (8 ounces) sliced water chestnuts, drained and halved

Direction

- Pour a bit of water into a saucepan followed by Brussels sprouts, steaming them with the cover on for around 12 to 14 minutes until they tenderize. Mix pepper, salt, dill, lemon juice, mustard and butter together. After draining Brussels sprouts, insert the water chestnuts and butter mixture. Stir until thoroughly mixed.

Nutrition Information

- Calories: 121 calories
- Protein: 4g protein.
- Total Fat: 6g fat (4g saturated fat)
- Sodium: 230mg sodium
- Fiber: 5g fiber)
- Total Carbohydrate: 15g carbohydrate (4g sugars
- Cholesterol: 15mg cholesterol

58. Dumplings With Tomatoes And Zucchini

Serving: 6 servings. | Prep: 5mins | Ready in:

Ingredients

- 1/4 cups chopped onion
- 2 tablespoons vegetable oil
- 4 large fresh tomatoes, peeled and chopped
- 1 tablespoon minced fresh basil or 1 teaspoon dried basil
- 1 teaspoon sugar
- 1 teaspoon salt
- 1/4 teaspoon pepper
- 2 medium zucchini, peeled and cubed
- PARMESAN DUMPLINGS:
- 1 egg, lightly beaten
- 1 cup grated Parmesan cheese

Direction

- Saute onion in a big skillet with oil until soft. Put in pepper, salt, sugar, basil and tomatoes, then simmer with a cover about 10 minutes. Put in zucchini and cook with a cover until soft, about 15 minutes. To make dumplings, mix cheese and egg together. Drop on tomato mixture by tablespoons. Simmer with a cover until dumplings become firm, about 5 minutes.

Nutrition Information

- Calories: 153 calories
- Protein: 8g protein.
- Total Fat: 10g fat (3g saturated fat)
- Sodium: 665mg sodium
- Fiber: 2g fiber)
- Total Carbohydrate: 9g carbohydrate (6g sugars
- Cholesterol: 46mg cholesterol

59. Easy German Biscuits

Serving: 15 biscuits. | Prep: 20mins | Ready in:

Ingredients

- 1 package (1/4 ounce) active dry yeast
- 1/2 cup warm water (110° to 115°)
- 2-1/2 cups all-purpose flour
- 1/3 cup sugar
- 2 teaspoons baking powder
- 1 teaspoon salt
- 1/4 teaspoon baking soda
- 1 cup buttermilk
- 1/4 cup vegetable oil

Direction

- In warm water, dissolve yeast. Mix baking soda, salt, baking powder, sugar and flour in a big bowl. Put in oil, buttermilk and yeast mixture; mix them well. Keep it covered and let chill in the refrigerator for no less than 12 hours. Punch down. Turn out onto a surface which is floured and roll out to 1 inch in thickness. Chop using a 2-inch biscuit cutter and position 2 inches apart on a baking sheet which is greased. Bake at 400 degrees for 12 minutes.

Nutrition Information

- Calories: 133 calories
- Fiber: 1g fiber)
- Total Carbohydrate: 21g carbohydrate (5g sugars
- Cholesterol: 1mg cholesterol
- Protein: 3g protein.
- Total Fat: 4g fat (1g saturated fat)
- Sodium: 249mg sodium

60. Easy Sauerkraut Salad

Serving: 8-10 servings. | Prep: 15mins | Ready in:

Ingredients

- 1 can (27 ounces) sauerkraut, rinsed and drained
- 1 cup finely chopped celery
- 1 cup finely chopped onion
- 1 jar (2 ounces) chopped pimientos, drained
- 1 cup sugar

Direction

- Mix the first 4 ingredients together in a big bowl, then drizzle over with sugar and blend well. Cover and chill overnight, then serve cold.

Nutrition Information

- Calories: 101 calories
- Protein: 1g protein.
- Total Fat: 0 fat (0 saturated fat)
- Sodium: 518mg sodium
- Fiber: 3g fiber)
- Total Carbohydrate: 25g carbohydrate (21g sugars
- Cholesterol: 0 cholesterol

61. Fancy Brussels Sprouts

Serving: 6 servings. | Prep: 15mins | Ready in:

Ingredients

- 1 cup water
- 1/4 cup minced fresh parsley
- 1 teaspoon sugar
- 1/2 teaspoon salt, optional
- 2 pints fresh brussels sprouts or 4 cups frozen brussels sprouts, thawed
- 1 can (8 ounces) water chestnuts, drained and diced
- 1 tablespoon butter

Direction

- Put sugar, parsley and water into a big saucepan. If using, add salt. Lead it to boiling point at medium heat. Insert the Brussels sprouts and lead it to boiling point. Lower the heat, leave it simmering with the cover on until they tenderize or for around 6 to 8 minutes before draining. Insert the butter and water chestnuts, cooking until thoroughly heated.

Nutrition Information

- Calories: 67 calories
- Total Fat: 2g fat (0 saturated fat)
- Sodium: 34mg sodium
- Fiber: 0 fiber)

- Total Carbohydrate: 11g carbohydrate (0 sugars
- Cholesterol: 0 cholesterol
- Protein: 3g protein. Diabetic Exchanges: 2 vegetable

62. Fast Lemony Brussels Sprouts

Serving: 4 servings. | Prep: 15mins | Ready in:

Ingredients

- 1 pound fresh brussels sprouts, trimmed and halved
- 2 tablespoons water
- 2 tablespoons butter, melted
- 2 tablespoons lemon juice
- 2 teaspoons grated lemon peel
- 1/4 teaspoon salt
- 1/4 teaspoon lemon-pepper seasoning
- 1/4 cup sliced almonds, toasted

Direction

- In a dish that's safe for the microwave, insert the Brussels sprouts and pour in water. For the next 7 to 9 minutes, start cooking on high with a cover on until the sprouts tenderize. During the process, stir it two times. After draining, finish off by stirring in the lemon-pepper, salt, peel, lemon juice and butter then sprinkling almonds over the top.

Nutrition Information

- Calories: 113 calories
- Total Carbohydrate: 12g carbohydrate (0 sugars
- Cholesterol: 0 cholesterol
- Protein: 5g protein. Diabetic Exchanges: 2 vegetable
- Total Fat: 6g fat (1g saturated fat)
- Sodium: 263mg sodium
- Fiber: 5g fiber)

63. Flavorful Coleslaw

Serving: 6-8 servings. | Prep: 20mins | Ready in:

Ingredients

- 3 cups shredded cabbage
- 3 cups shredded red cabbage
- 1 large unpeeled Granny Smith apple, shredded
- 1/2 cup finely chopped celery
- 1/4 cup finely chopped onion
- DRESSING:
- 1/2 cup mayonnaise
- 2 tablespoons sugar
- 1 tablespoon prepared mustard
- Salt and pepper to taste

Direction

- Properly mix onion, celery, apple and cabbage in a large bowl. Mix well. Mix the ingredients for dressing in a separate small bowl, add it to the coleslaw and mix. Chill for a few hours, then serve.

Nutrition Information

- Calories: 145 calories
- Sodium: 110mg sodium
- Fiber: 2g fiber)
- Total Carbohydrate: 11g carbohydrate (8g sugars
- Cholesterol: 5mg cholesterol
- Protein: 1g protein.
- Total Fat: 11g fat (2g saturated fat)

64. Floret Cheese Strudel

Serving: 2 strudels (4-6 servings each). | Prep: 30mins | Ready in:

Ingredients

- 3-1/2 cups broccoli florets
- 2-1/2 cups caulifloweret
- 1 small onion, chopped
- 1 garlic clove, minced
- 6 tablespoons butter, divided
- 2 tablespoons all-purpose flour
- 1 cup whole milk
- 2 tablespoons grated Parmesan cheese
- 1 package (17-1/4 ounces) frozen puff pastry, thawed
- 1 cup shredded mozzarella cheese
- 1/2 cup shredded cheddar cheese

Direction

- Place cauliflower and broccoli in a big saucepan, pour in 1 inch of water and heat to a boil. Decrease heat, put on a cover and allow to simmer until crisp-tender, 5-10 minutes. Drain; put aside.
- Sauté garlic and onion in 2 tablespoons butter in a big saucepan, until tender. Mix in flour until combined; slowly pour in milk. Heat to a boil; stir and cook until thick, about 2 minutes. Take away from heat. Mix in cauliflower, broccoli, and Parmesan cheese; put aside.
- Melt the rest of butter. Arrange a sheet of puff pastry over a piece of waxed paper; brush butter over the surface. With a spoon, spread 1/2 of vegetable mixture along 1 long side of pastry. Sprinkle with cheddar and mozzarella cheeses. Roll up jelly-roll style, beginning from the long side topped with vegetable mixture; pinch ends and seams to seal. Brush melted butter over top. Be careful to place the seam side down on an unoiled baking tray. Repeat with the rest of vegetable mixture and dough.
- Bake at 400 degrees until golden brown, 20-25 minutes. Let sit 5 minutes. Use a serrated knife to cut.

Nutrition Information

- Calories: 327 calories
- Protein: 8g protein.
- Total Fat: 21g fat (9g saturated fat)
- Sodium: 293mg sodium
- Fiber: 4g fiber)
- Total Carbohydrate: 28g carbohydrate (2g sugars
- Cholesterol: 31mg cholesterol

65. Fried Apples And Onions

Serving: 8 servings. | Prep: 15mins | Ready in:

Ingredients

- 6 medium onions, sliced and separated into rings
- 2 tablespoons butter
- 6 medium tart red apples, cut into 1/4-inch wedges
- 3 tablespoons brown sugar

Direction

- Put butter and onions in a large skillet then cook on medium heat for 3 to 5 minutes or until onions become crisp-tender. Put apples on top, use brown sugar to sprinkle. Put a lid on and cook for 15 to 20 minutes or till apples become soft.

Nutrition Information

- Calories: 151 calories
- Protein: 2g protein.
- Total Fat: 3g fat (2g saturated fat)
- Sodium: 35mg sodium
- Fiber: 5g fiber)
- Total Carbohydrate: 31g carbohydrate (24g sugars
- Cholesterol: 8mg cholesterol

66. Garlic Brussels Sprouts

Serving: 1 serving. | Prep: 5mins | Ready in:

Ingredients

- 5 brussels sprouts, halved
- 1 garlic clove, minced
- 1 teaspoon butter, melted
- 1 tablespoon shredded Parmesan cheese, optional

Direction

- In a small saucepan, insert the garlic, Brussels sprouts and an inch of water. Lead it to boiling point then lower the heat. Leave it simmering with the cover on for 6 to 8 minutes or until the sprouts are crispy and tender before draining. Add butter in a drizzling motion. If desired, scatter Parmesan cheese.

Nutrition Information

- Calories: 79 calories
- Total Fat: 4g fat (2g saturated fat)
- Sodium: 63mg sodium
- Fiber: 4g fiber)
- Total Carbohydrate: 10g carbohydrate (2g sugars
- Cholesterol: 10mg cholesterol
- Protein: 3g protein.

67. German Apple Cake With Sweet Drizzle

Serving: 10 servings. | Prep: 25mins | Ready in:

Ingredients

- 1/2 cup butter, softened
- 2/3 cup sugar
- 2 eggs
- 4 teaspoons milk
- 1/8 teaspoon lemon extract
- 2 cups all-purpose flour
- 2-1/2 teaspoons baking powder
- 1/8 teaspoon salt
- 2 medium tart apples, peeled and thinly sliced
- 1 cup confectioners' sugar
- 2 tablespoons butter, softened
- 2 to 3 teaspoons milk

Direction

- Cream sugar and butter together in a big bowl until fluffy and light. Put in eggs and blend well. Beat in extract and milk. Mix together salt, baking powder and flour, then beat flour mixture into creamed mixture just until blended. Pat the dough into a 9-inch springform pan coated with grease using your hands coated lightly with flour. Place on top of dough with apples.
- Bake at 350 degrees until a toothpick exits clean after being inserted in the center, about 40 to 50 minutes. Allow to cool on wire rack about 10 minutes prior to taking out of pan. Mix together milk, butter and confectioners' sugar, then drizzle over top.

Nutrition Information

- Calories: 325 calories
- Sodium: 226mg sodium
- Fiber: 1g fiber)
- Total Carbohydrate: 49g carbohydrate (29g sugars
- Cholesterol: 73mg cholesterol
- Protein: 4g protein.
- Total Fat: 13g fat (8g saturated fat)

68. German Apple Pancake

Serving: 4 | Prep: 15mins | Ready in:

Ingredients

- 4 eggs

- 1/2 cup unbleached all-purpose flour
- 1/2 teaspoon baking powder
- 1 tablespoon sugar
- 1 pinch salt
- 1 cup milk
- 1 teaspoon vanilla extract
- 2 tablespoons unsalted butter, melted
- 1/2 teaspoon ground nutmeg
- 1/4 cup unsalted butter
- 1/2 cup white sugar, divided
- 1/2 teaspoon ground cinnamon
- 1/2 teaspoon ground nutmeg
- 1 large tart apple - peeled, cored and sliced

Direction

- Whisk eggs, sugar, salt, flour, and baking powder in a large bowl. Slowly stir in milk, little by little, while stirring the mixture constantly. Add melted butter, 1/2 tsp. of nutmeg, and vanilla. Allow the batter to stand for 30 minutes or overnight.
- Set the oven to 425°F (220°C) for preheating.
- Brush and melt butter on all sides of the 10-inch oven proof skillet. Combine 1/2 tsp. of nutmeg, 1/4 cup of sugar, and cinnamon in a small bowl, and then pour it all over the butter. Arrange apple slices into the skillet, and top it with the remaining sugar. Place the skillet over medium-high heat and heat until the mixture starts to form bubbles. Slowly pour the batter over the hot apples.
- Let it bake inside the preheated oven for 15 minutes. Adjust the heat to 375°F (190°C) and let it bake for 10 more minutes. Before serving, cut the pancakes into wedges and place them on a serving platter.

Nutrition Information

- Calories: 456 calories;
- Protein: 10.3
- Total Fat: 24
- Sodium: 143
- Total Carbohydrate: 51.5
- Cholesterol: 237

69. German Beer Cheese Spread

Serving: 2-1/2 cups. | Prep: 15mins | Ready in:

Ingredients

- 1 pound sharp cheddar cheese, cut into 1/2-inch cubes
- 1 tablespoon Worcestershire sauce
- 1-1/2 teaspoons prepared mustard
- 1 small garlic clove, minced
- 1/4 teaspoon salt
- 1/8 teaspoon pepper
- 2/3 cup German beer or nonalcoholic beer
- Assorted crackers or vegetables

Direction

- In a food processor, add cheese and process for 1 minute until chopped finely. Put in pepper, salt, garlic, mustard and Worcestershire sauce, then pour beer into the mixture slowly while keep on processing for 1 1/2 minutes, until the mixture is spreadable and smooth.
- Turn to gift jars or a serving bowl. Chill with a cover for up to 1 week. Serve together with crackers or vegetables.

Nutrition Information

- Calories: 95 calories
- Fiber: 0 fiber)
- Total Carbohydrate: 1g carbohydrate (0 sugars
- Cholesterol: 24mg cholesterol
- Protein: 6g protein.
- Total Fat: 8g fat (5g saturated fat)
- Sodium: 187mg sodium

70. German Chocolate Ring

Serving: 24 servings. | Prep: 30mins | Ready in:

Ingredients

- 1-1/4 cups sweetened shredded coconut, divided
- 1 cup (6 ounces) semisweet chocolate chips, divided
- 3/4 cup chopped pecans
- 3 large eggs, divided use
- 4-1/2 to 5 cups all-purpose flour
- 1/2 cup sugar
- 1 teaspoon salt
- 1 package (1/4 ounce) active dry yeast
- 1 cup whole milk
- 5 tablespoons butter, divided

Direction

- Mix 1 egg, pecans, 3/4 cup of chocolate chips and a cup of coconut in small bowl; reserve. Mix yeast, salt, sugar and a cup of flour in big bowl. Heat 4 tablespoons of butter and milk in small saucepan to 120° to 130°; put into the flour mixture, whipping till smooth. Put in the rest of the eggs and sufficient leftover flour to make a soft dough.
- Transfer to a slightly floured area; knead for 6 to 8 minutes, till elastic and smooth. Put in an oiled bowl, flipping one time to oil the surface. Put on a cover; allow to rise in warm area till doubled, about an hour.
- Punch down the dough; transfer to a slightly floured area. Roll the dough into rectangle, 18x10-inch in size. Liquify the rest of the butter and brush on dough; scatter with the reserved mixture of chocolate.
- Beginning with a long side, roll dough up like jelly-roll; press seam to seal. Put on oiled baking sheet, seam side facing down. Press ends together to make a ring.
- Cut from outer edge using scissors to 2/3 of the way toward the middle of ring at an-inch intervals. Slightly part the strips; twist to let filling show. Put on a cover and allow to rise till doubled, about an hour.
- Bake till golden brown, about 20 to 25 minutes at 350°. Scatter with the rest of chocolate chips; allow to rest for 5 minutes. Scatter with liquified chips; scatter with the rest of coconut. Cautiously transfer from the pan to the wire rack to let cool.

Nutrition Information

- Calories: 222 calories
- Total Fat: 10g fat (5g saturated fat)
- Sodium: 149mg sodium
- Fiber: 2g fiber)
- Total Carbohydrate: 30g carbohydrate (11g sugars
- Cholesterol: 34mg cholesterol
- Protein: 4g protein.

71. German Coleslaw

Serving: 14-18 servings. | Prep: 10mins | Ready in:

Ingredients

- 1 medium head cabbage, finely shredded
- 3 to 4 green onions, sliced
- 3/4 cup sugar
- 3/4 cup vinegar
- 1-1/2 teaspoons celery seed
- 1-1/2 teaspoons salt
- 3/4 cup canola oil

Direction

- Mix the onions and the cabbage together in a big bowl. Mix the salt, celery seed, vinegar and sugar in a saucepan. Let it boil. Put in oil. Keep it boiling until the sugar is dissolved. Put in the cabbage and toss it gently. Let it chill.

Nutrition Information

- Calories: 126 calories

- Total Carbohydrate: 11g carbohydrate (9g sugars
- Cholesterol: 0 cholesterol
- Protein: 1g protein.
- Total Fat: 9g fat (1g saturated fat)
- Sodium: 206mg sodium
- Fiber: 1g fiber)

72. German Cucumber Salad

Serving: 4-6 servings. | Prep: 10mins | Ready in:

Ingredients

- 2 medium cucumbers, thinly sliced
- 4 green onions, thinly sliced
- 3 small tomatoes, sliced
- 2 tablespoons fresh snipped parsley
- DRESSING:
- 1/4 cup sour cream
- 1/4 teaspoon prepared mustard
- 2 tablespoons minced fresh dill
- 1 tablespoon white vinegar
- 1 tablespoon milk
- 1/8 teaspoon pepper

Direction

- Combine parsley, tomatoes, onions, and cucumbers in a bowl. Mix dressing ingredients together; pour on cucumber mixture and gently toss. Cover and let chill for at least an hour.

Nutrition Information

- Calories: 50 calories
- Fiber: 2g fiber)
- Total Carbohydrate: 6g carbohydrate (4g sugars
- Cholesterol: 7mg cholesterol
- Protein: 2g protein.
- Total Fat: 2g fat (1g saturated fat)
- Sodium: 15mg sodium

73. German Cukes And Tomatoes

Serving: 8 servings. | Prep: 20mins | Ready in:

Ingredients

- 2 medium cucumbers, thinly sliced
- 4 green onions, thinly sliced
- 2 tablespoons minced fresh parsley
- 1/4 cup sour cream
- 2 tablespoons snipped fresh dill
- 1 tablespoon cider vinegar
- 1/2 teaspoon salt
- 1/4 teaspoon prepared mustard
- 1/8 teaspoon pepper
- 1 tablespoon milk, optional
- 3 small tomatoes, sliced

Direction

- In a large bowl, combine the parsley, onions and cucumbers. In a small bowl, combine the dill, sour cream, salt, vinegar, pepper and mustard. Add in milk if you want to make a thinner dressing. Pour over cucumber mixture and coat by tossing. Divide among eight salad plates; place tomatoes on top.

Nutrition Information

- Calories: 37 calories
- Sodium: 158mg sodium
- Fiber: 1g fiber)
- Total Carbohydrate: 5g carbohydrate (3g sugars
- Cholesterol: 5mg cholesterol
- Protein: 1g protein. Diabetic Exchanges: 1 vegetable
- Total Fat: 1g fat (1g saturated fat)

74. German Noodle Bake

Serving: 8 servings. | Prep: 45mins | Ready in:

Ingredients

- 1 cup all-purpose flour
- 1/2 teaspoon salt
- 2 large eggs, lightly beaten
- 2 quarts water
- CHEESE SAUCE:
- 3 tablespoons butter
- 3 tablespoons all-purpose flour
- 1/2 teaspoon salt
- 1/2 teaspoon paprika
- 1-1/2 cups milk
- 8 ounces Swiss cheese, diced
- 2 large eggs, well beaten

Direction

- Mix the salt and flour in a small bowl. Create a well in the center; add the eggs. Stir until it forms a dough.
- On a floured surface, place the dough; knead for 5-6 minutes. Divide the dough in half. Roll each portion into a 12x9-inch rectangle. Sprinkle the flour over both sides of the dough; roll up, jelly-roll style. Slice into 1/4-inch slices. On the paper towels, unroll the noodles; dry for 2 hours.
- Set the oven to 350 degrees and start preheating. Rapid boil water in a Dutch oven. Add noodles; cook until tender for 7-9 minutes.
- At the same time, let the butter melt in a small saucepan. Stir in paprika, salt, and flour until smooth; slowly pour in the milk. Allow to boil; stir and cook until thick for 2 minutes. Take away from the heat; add cheese and stir until melted. Add eggs and stir.
- Let the noodles drain; transfer into a greased 11x7-inch baking dish. Put cheese sauce on top. Bake, covered, for 20 minutes. Uncover and bake until bubbly for 10-15 minutes more.

Nutrition Information

- Calories: 275 calories
- Fiber: 1g fiber)
- Total Carbohydrate: 17g carbohydrate (4g sugars
- Cholesterol: 148mg cholesterol
- Protein: 15g protein.
- Total Fat: 16g fat (9g saturated fat)
- Sodium: 453mg sodium

75. German Pancake

Serving: 8 servings (2 cups syrup). | Prep: 10mins | Ready in:

Ingredients

- 6 large eggs
- 1 cup 2% milk
- 1 cup all-purpose flour
- 1/2 teaspoon salt
- 2 tablespoons butter, melted
- BUTTERMILK SYRUP:
- 1/2 cup butter, cubed
- 1-1/2 cups sugar
- 3/4 cup buttermilk
- 2 tablespoons corn syrup
- 1 teaspoon baking soda
- 2 teaspoons vanilla extract
- Confectioners' sugar
- Fresh blueberries, optional

Direction

- Turn on the oven and preheat to 400°F. Blend the first four ingredients in a blender until smooth.
- Melt butter and pour it into a 13x9-inch baking dish, tilting it to coat all sides. Add the batter and bake it uncovered for 20 minutes until golden brown and puffed.
- While waiting, combine baking soda, buttermilk, butter, corn syrup, and sugar in a small saucepan. Bring the mixture to boil and cook it uncovered for 7 minutes. Remove the mixture from heat and add vanilla; mix it well.

- Remove the baked pancake from the oven and sprinkle confectioners' sugar on its top. You can serve it with syrup of fresh blueberries if desired.

Nutrition Information

- Calories: 428 calories
- Cholesterol: 203mg cholesterol
- Protein: 8g protein.
- Total Fat: 19g fat (11g saturated fat)
- Sodium: 543mg sodium
- Fiber: 0 fiber)
- Total Carbohydrate: 56g carbohydrate (42g sugars

76. German Potato Balls

Serving: 10 servings. | Prep: 50mins | Ready in:

Ingredients

- 3 pounds russet potatoes
- 2 eggs
- 1 cup all-purpose flour, divided
- 1/2 cup dry bread crumbs
- 1 teaspoon salt
- 1/4 teaspoon ground nutmeg
- Dash pepper
- Minced fresh parsley, optional

Direction

- In a saucepan, add potatoes and water to cover, then bring to a boil. Lower heat and simmer with a cover until softened, about 30 to 35 minutes. Drain well and chill about 2 hours to overnight.
- Peel potatoes and grate them. Mix together pepper, nutmeg, salt, bread crumbs, 3/4 cup of flour and eggs in a bowl, then put in potatoes. Use your hands to mix together until well combined. Form the mixture into balls, 1 1/2 inches size, then roll balls into leftover flour.
- Bring salted water in a big kettle to a boil. Put into boiling water with several dumplings at a time, then simmer without a cover until dumplings rise to the top. Cook for 2 minutes more. Use slotted spoon to take dumplings out and put into a serving bowl. Sprinkle parsley over cooked dumplings if you want.

Nutrition Information

- Calories: 190 calories
- Protein: 6g protein.
- Total Fat: 2g fat (0 saturated fat)
- Sodium: 304mg sodium
- Fiber: 3g fiber)
- Total Carbohydrate: 38g carbohydrate (3g sugars
- Cholesterol: 43mg cholesterol

77. German Potato Dumplings

Serving: 8 servings. | Prep: 40mins | Ready in:

Ingredients

- 3 pounds medium potatoes (about 10), peeled and quartered
- 1 cup all-purpose flour
- 3 eggs, lightly beaten
- 2/3 cup dry bread crumbs
- 1 teaspoon salt
- 1/2 teaspoon ground nutmeg
- 12 cups water
- BROWNED BUTTER SAUCE:
- 1/2 cup butter, cubed
- 1 tablespoon chopped onion
- 1/4 cup dry bread crumbs

Direction

- In a Dutch oven, place potatoes and pour water to cover. Boil, lower the heat; uncover and cook until softened, around 15-20 minutes. Allow to drain and transfer to a large bowl.

- Next, mash the potatoes. Stir in nutmeg, salt, bread crumbs, eggs, and flour. Roll into 16 balls (2-in. in size).
- Boil 12 cups water in a Dutch oven. Add dumplings carefully. Reduce the heat; simmer for 7-9 minutes, uncovered, or until a toothpick comes out clean from the middle of the dumplings.
- In the meantime, heat onion and butter over medium heat in a small heavy saucepan, until the butter is golden brown, about 5-7 minutes, stirring continuously. Next, remove from the heat and stir in the bread crumbs. Enjoy with dumplings.

Nutrition Information

- Calories: 367 calories
- Sodium: 524mg sodium
- Fiber: 5g fiber)
- Total Carbohydrate: 51g carbohydrate (2g sugars
- Cholesterol: 100mg cholesterol
- Protein: 9g protein.
- Total Fat: 14g fat (8g saturated fat)

78. German Potato Patties

Serving: 2 servings. | Prep: 10mins | Ready in:

Ingredients

- 1-1/3 cups finely shredded russet potatoes, squeezed dry
- 1 small onion, finely chopped
- 2 tablespoons chopped celery
- 1 egg, lightly beaten
- 1 tablespoon minced fresh parsley
- 1/2 teaspoon salt
- 1/2 teaspoon minced fresh marjoram or 1/8 teaspoon dried marjoram
- 1/8 teaspoon curry powder
- 1/8 teaspoon caraway seeds
- 1/8 teaspoon paprika
- Dash pepper
- 1-1/2 teaspoons canola oil, divided

Direction

- Mix the first eleven ingredients together in a big bowl. Heat 3/4 tsp. of oil in a big nonstick skillet coated with cooking spray on medium heat. Drop into skillet the potato mixture by 1/4 cupfuls, then press slightly to flatten. Fry until turn golden brown, about 3 to 4 minutes per side. Do the same process with leftover potato mixture and oil.

Nutrition Information

- Calories: 200 calories
- Cholesterol: 106mg cholesterol
- Protein: 7g protein.
- Total Fat: 7g fat (1g saturated fat)
- Sodium: 661mg sodium
- Fiber: 3g fiber)
- Total Carbohydrate: 29g carbohydrate (3g sugars

79. German Potato Soup

Serving: 6 servings. | Prep: 10mins | Ready in:

Ingredients

- 6 cups cubed peeled potatoes
- 1-1/4 cups sliced celery
- 1/2 cup chopped onion
- 5 cups water
- 1/2 teaspoon salt
- 1/8 teaspoon pepper
- Butter
- Minced fresh parsley
- DROP DUMPLINGS:
- 1 large egg, beaten

- 1/3 cup water
- 1/2 teaspoon salt
- 3/4 cup all-purpose flour

Direction

- In a Dutch oven, mix the first six ingredients; boil. Lessen heat; simmer while covered for 1 hour or until vegetables turn soft.
- Use a potato masher to puree nearly all the vegetables. For dumplings, stir in the flour, salt, water and egg till stiff and smooth. Drop by teaspoonfuls into the boiling soup. Simmer while covered for about 10 minutes until cooked completely. Top each serving with parsley and a butter.

Nutrition Information

- Calories: 213 calories
- Sodium: 434mg sodium
- Fiber: 4g fiber)
- Total Carbohydrate: 45g carbohydrate (3g sugars
- Cholesterol: 35mg cholesterol
- Protein: 6g protein.
- Total Fat: 1g fat (0 saturated fat)

80. German Red Cabbage

Serving: 10 servings. | Prep: 10mins | Ready in:

Ingredients

- 1 medium onion, halved and sliced
- 1 medium apple, sliced
- 1 medium head red cabbage, shredded (about 8 cups)
- 1/3 cup sugar
- 1/3 cup white vinegar
- 3/4 teaspoon salt, optional
- 1/4 teaspoon pepper

Direction

- Cook and stir apple and onion in a big Dutch oven coated with cooking spray on moderate heat for 5 minutes, until onion is softened. Stir in the leftover ingredients; then cook for an hour with a cover while stirring sometimes, until cabbage is softened. Serve warm or chilled.

Nutrition Information

- Calories: 64 calories
- Protein: 1g protein. Diabetic Exchanges: 1 vegetable
- Total Fat: 0 fat (0 saturated fat)
- Sodium: 23mg sodium
- Fiber: 2g fiber)
- Total Carbohydrate: 16g carbohydrate (12g sugars
- Cholesterol: 0 cholesterol

81. German Rye Bread

Serving: 24 | Prep: | Ready in:

Ingredients

- 2 (.25 ounce) packages active dry yeast
- 1/2 cup warm water (110 degrees F/45 degrees C)
- 1 1/2 cups lukewarm milk
- 2 tablespoons white sugar
- 1 teaspoon salt
- 1/2 cup molasses
- 2 tablespoons butter
- 3 1/4 cups rye flour
- 2 1/2 cups bread flour

Direction

- In a warm water, dissolve yeast.
- Mix together salt, sugar, and milk in a big bowl. With a mixer, beat in a cup of rye flour, yeast mixture, butter, and molasses.

- Mix in the rest of the rye flour using a wooden spoon. Stir in the white flour until the dough becomes stiff enough to knead.
- Knead the dough, adding flour as necessary, for about 5 minutes to 10. Add more flour if the dough sticks to the board or to your hands.
- Put on cover and allow the dough to rise until it doubles, about 1 to 1 and a half hour.
- Press down the dough and divide into two round loaves. Allow loaves to rise on an oiled baking sheet for about 1 and a half hour until the size doubles.
- Set oven to 190°C (375°F) and bake the loaves for 30 to 35 minutes.

Nutrition Information

- Calories: 144 calories;
- Sodium: 113
- Total Carbohydrate: 28.5
- Cholesterol: 4
- Protein: 3.6
- Total Fat: 1.7

82. German Stollen

Serving: 24 | Prep: 30mins | Ready in:

Ingredients

- 8 cups all-purpose flour
- 3 ounces compressed fresh yeast
- 1 pinch white sugar
- 1 tablespoon lukewarm milk
- 1 1/2 cups milk
- 1 cup unsalted butter
- 2 tablespoons unsalted butter
- 1 cup white sugar
- 2 egg yolks
- 1/2 teaspoon salt
- 1 3/4 cups chopped blanched almonds
- 1 1/4 cups raisins
- 6 tablespoons candied lemon peel
- 6 tablespoons chopped candied orange peel
- 2 tablespoons melted butter
- 2 tablespoons confectioners' sugar

Direction

- In a big bowl, put the flour; create a well in the middle and break up fresh yeast into it. Scatter sugar over and put in a tablespoon of milk. Place a cover and allow to rise for 15 minutes at warm area.
- In saucepan on low heat, heat a cup plus 2 tablespoons of unsalted butter and 1 1/2 cups of milk till butter melts.
- On top of yeast mixture, put the milk-butter mixture; put in salt, egg yolks and a cup of sugar. Knead till a soft dough forms. Put on a clean dish towel to cover and allow to rise in warm area till doubled in size for an hour.
- Line parchment paper on a baking sheet.
- Stir together the candied orange peel, candied lemon peel, raisins and almonds, then fold into dough. Form dough into loaf and put onto the prepped baking sheet. Place a cover and allow to rest till loaf has risen slightly once more for half an hour.
- Preheat the oven to 190°C or 375°F.
- In the prepped oven, bake for 45 minutes to an hour till toothpick pricked in the center comes out clean. Take out of the oven. Immediately brush 2 tablespoons of melted butter on hot stollen and sprinkle with confectioners' sugar.

Nutrition Information

- Calories: 395 calories;
- Cholesterol: 44
- Protein: 8
- Total Fat: 16.1
- Sodium: 73
- Total Carbohydrate: 56.8

83. German Style Pickled Eggs

Serving: 12 servings. | Prep: 10mins | Ready in:

Ingredients

- 2 cups cider vinegar
- 1 cup sugar
- 1/2 cup water
- 2 tablespoons prepared mustard
- 1 tablespoon salt
- 1 tablespoon celery seed
- 1 tablespoon mustard seed
- 6 whole cloves
- 2 medium onions, thinly sliced
- 12 hard-boiled large eggs, peeled

Direction

- Mix the first 8 ingredients together in a big saucepan. Boil. Lower the heat, put a cover on and simmer for 10 minutes. Let cool down fully. In a big jar, put eggs and onions, and fill with enough vinegar mixture to cover entirely. Put a cover on and chill for a minimum of 8 hours or overnight. Every time taking out the eggs for serving, use a clean spoon. Chill for a maximum of 1 week.

Nutrition Information

- Calories: 166 calories
- Sodium: 682mg sodium
- Fiber: 1g fiber)
- Total Carbohydrate: 23g carbohydrate (21g sugars
- Cholesterol: 212mg cholesterol
- Protein: 7g protein.
- Total Fat: 6g fat (2g saturated fat)

84. Gingerbread Muffins

Serving: 1 dozen (1 cup lemon curd). | Prep: 45mins | Ready in:

Ingredients

- LEMON CURD:
- 2/3 cup sugar
- 3/4 teaspoon cornstarch
- 1/3 cup lemon juice
- 5 large egg yolks, lightly beaten
- 1/4 cup butter, cubed
- 2 teaspoons grated lemon peel
- MUFFINS:
- 2 cups all-purpose flour
- 1/4 cup sugar
- 2-1/2 teaspoons baking powder
- 2 teaspoons ground ginger
- 1 teaspoon ground cinnamon
- 1/4 teaspoon salt
- 1/4 teaspoon ground cloves
- 1 large egg
- 3/4 cup whole milk
- 1/4 cup canola oil
- 1/4 cup molasses

Direction

- Mix together lemon juice, cornstarch and sugar in a big heavy saucepan until smooth. Cook and stir the mixture on moderately high heat until bubbly and thickened. Lower heat to low then cook and stir for 2 minutes more. Take away from the heat. Stir into egg yolks with some of the hot filling, then turn all back to pan while stirring continuously. Bring the mixture to a gentle boil, then cook and stir about 2 minutes. Take away from the heat and stir in lemon peel and butter gently until combined. Transfer into a big bowl and use plastic wrap to cover the surface. Cover and chill until ready to serve.
- Mix together cloves, salt, cinnamon, ginger, baking powder, sugar and flour in a big bowl. Mix together molasses, oil, milk and egg in a separate bowl until smooth, then stir into flour mixture just until blended.
- Fill batter into muffin cups lined with paper until 1/2 full. Bake at 375 degrees until a toothpick exits clean after being inserted in the center, about 15 to 20 minutes. Allow to cool about 5 minutes prior to transferring from pan to a wire rack. Serve warm together with lemon curd.

Nutrition Information

- Calories: 271 calories
- Sodium: 190mg sodium
- Fiber: 1g fiber)
- Total Carbohydrate: 38g carbohydrate (20g sugars
- Cholesterol: 119mg cholesterol
- Protein: 4g protein.
- Total Fat: 12g fat (4g saturated fat)

85. Gingerbread Oatmeal Bread

Serving: 1 loaf (16 slices). | Prep: 10mins | Ready in:

Ingredients

- 1 cup plus 1 tablespoon water (70° to 80°)
- 1/2 cup molasses
- 1 tablespoon canola oil
- 3 cups bread flour
- 1 cup old-fashioned oats
- 1-1/2 teaspoons ground cinnamon
- 1 to 1-1/2 teaspoons ground ginger
- 1 teaspoon salt
- 1/2 teaspoon grated orange zest
- 1/4 teaspoon ground nutmeg
- 1/4 teaspoon ground cloves
- 1 package (1/4 ounce) active dry yeast

Direction

- Measure all ingredients in the pan of the bread machine in order manufacturer recommended. Choose basic bread setting. If available, choose loaf size and crust color. Follow to bread machine directions to bake (after 5 minutes of mixing, check dough; if needed add 1 to 2 tablespoons of bread flour or water).

Nutrition Information

- Calories: 131 calories
- Total Fat: 1g fat (0 saturated fat)
- Sodium: 152mg sodium
- Fiber: 1g fiber)
- Total Carbohydrate: 27g carbohydrate (6g sugars
- Cholesterol: 0 cholesterol
- Protein: 4g protein. Diabetic Exchanges: 2 starch.

86. Gingerbread Pancakes

Serving: 9 | Prep: 15mins | Ready in:

Ingredients

- 3 cups all-purpose flour
- 6 tablespoons baking powder
- 3 teaspoons unsweetened cocoa powder
- 1 1/2 teaspoons ground ginger
- 3/4 teaspoon ground cinnamon
- 3/4 teaspoon ground cloves
- 6 tablespoons ground hazelnuts
- 3 cups milk
- 6 egg whites
- 6 tablespoons dark molasses
- 6 tablespoons vegetable oil

Direction

- In a big bowl, sift together the flour, cocoa, cloves, ginger, baking powder and cinnamon. Mix in hazelnuts then put aside.
- In another bowl, beat together egg whites, molasses and milk.
- Create a well in the center of the dry ingredients and pour the egg mixture into it. Blend just enough to moisten and batter is lumpy.
- Set a lightly greased frying pan or griddle over medium high heat. Spoon batter onto the griddle, using about 1/4 cup for each pancake. Fry until brown on both sides. Serve while still hot.

Nutrition Information

- Calories: 359 calories;
- Protein: 10.3
- Total Fat: 14.2
- Sodium: 748
- Total Carbohydrate: 49.1
- Cholesterol: 7

87. Gingerbread Pancakes With Lemon Syrup

Serving: 10 pancakes (1-1/3 cups syrup). | Prep: 20mins | Ready in:

Ingredients

- 1-1/3 cups all-purpose flour
- 1 teaspoon baking powder
- 1 teaspoon ground cinnamon
- 1/2 teaspoon ground ginger
- 1/4 teaspoon baking soda
- 1/4 teaspoon salt
- 1 egg
- 1-1/4 cups milk
- 1/4 cup molasses
- 3 tablespoons vegetable oil
- LEMON SYRUP:
- 1/2 cup sugar
- 1 tablespoon cornstarch
- Pinch ground nutmeg
- 1 cup cold water
- 2 tablespoons butter, melted
- 2 tablespoons lemon juice
- 1/2 teaspoon grated lemon peel

Direction

- Mix salt, baking soda, ginger, cinnamon, baking powder and flour in a large bowl. Beat oil, molasses, milk and egg in another bowl. Add to the dry ingredients; beat just until they are blended.
- Pour batter by 1/4 cupful onto a greased hot griddle. Turn when bubbles appear on top of pancake; cook until the other side becomes golden brown.
- To make the syrup, in a saucepan, mix the nutmeg, cornstarch and sugar. Stir in water until it becomes smooth. Bring to a boil; cook while stirring until thickened or for 1-2 minutes. Take it away from the heat. Stir in butter, lemon peel and juice. Serve with pancakes.

Nutrition Information

- Calories: 417 calories
- Fiber: 1g fiber)
- Total Carbohydrate: 62g carbohydrate (33g sugars
- Cholesterol: 63mg cholesterol
- Protein: 7g protein.
- Total Fat: 16g fat (6g saturated fat)
- Sodium: 357mg sodium

88. Gingerbread Waffles

Serving: 4 | Prep: 20mins | Ready in:

Ingredients

- 1 tablespoon butter, softened
- 2 tablespoons molasses
- 1/4 cup liquid egg substitute
- 1/2 cup Kamut® flour
- 1/2 cup whole wheat pastry flour
- 1 teaspoon baking powder
- 1/4 teaspoon baking soda
- 1/8 teaspoon sea salt
- 1 teaspoon ground ginger
- 1/2 teaspoon cinnamon
- 1/8 teaspoon ground cloves
- 3/4 cup boiling water, or as needed

Direction

- Combine egg substitute, molasses and butter in a medium bowl, using an electric mixer until smooth. Stir cloves, cinnamon, ginger, salt, baking soda, baking powder, whole wheat flour and Kamut flour together in a separate bowl. Stir the flour mixture into the molasses mixture alternating with water, starting and finishing by the flour, while stirring just until combined.

- Preheat and coat the waffle iron with cooking spray. Scoop the wanted quantity of batter onto hot waffle iron and cook until waffles don't stick to the iron and steam stops coming out. Keep going with the leftover batter.

Nutrition Information

- Calories: 177 calories;
- Total Fat: 4.1
- Sodium: 308
- Total Carbohydrate: 29.7
- Cholesterol: 8
- Protein: 6

89. Glazed Brussels Sprouts

Serving: 5 servings. | Prep: 10mins | Ready in:

Ingredients

- 1 pound fresh brussels sprouts, halved
- 1/2 cup fresh baby carrots, halved
- 1 cup pecan halves
- 1/4 teaspoon chili powder
- 3 tablespoons butter
- 1/4 cup maple syrup
- 2 teaspoons cider vinegar
- 1/2 teaspoon salt

Direction

- In a big pot, put in carrots and Brussels sprouts; pour in enough water to cover then boil. Lower heat and let it simmer, covered, for 8mins until tender-crisp.
- Meanwhile, in a big pan, sauté chili powder and pecans in butter for two minutes. Drain veggies and place in the pecan mixture. Mix in salt, vinegar, and maple syrup. Cook for 3-5mins while continuously stirring until the sprouts are tender. Use a slotted spoon to serve.

Nutrition Information

- Calories: 296 calories
- Protein: 5g protein.
- Total Fat: 23g fat (6g saturated fat)
- Sodium: 321mg sodium
- Fiber: 6g fiber)
- Total Carbohydrate: 23g carbohydrate (13g sugars
- Cholesterol: 18mg cholesterol

90. Glazed Sprouts And Carrots

Serving: 4 servings. | Prep: 20mins | Ready in:

Ingredients

- 1/2 cup water
- 1 cup halved fresh Brussels sprouts
- 2 medium carrots, sliced
- 1 teaspoon cornstarch
- 1/2 teaspoon sugar
- 1/4 teaspoon salt
- 1/8 teaspoon ground nutmeg
- 1/3 cup orange juice

Direction

- Fill a big saucepan up with water. At moderate heat, lead it to a boil. Insert the vegetables. Leave them simmering with a cover on until they start tenderizing, about 6 to 8 minutes. After draining, put them back into the pan. Mix orange juice, nutmeg, sugar, corn-starch and salt if desired, stirring until combined and smooth. Empty this mixture out into the pan with vegetables. Lead it to boiling point, cooking and stirring until it thickens or for about 2 minutes.

Nutrition Information

- Calories: 37 calories
- Sodium: 176mg sodium
- Fiber: 2g fiber)
- Total Carbohydrate: 8g carbohydrate (4g sugars
- Cholesterol: 0 cholesterol
- Protein: 1g protein. Diabetic Exchanges: 1 vegetable.
- Total Fat: 0 fat (0 saturated fat)

91. Golden Caraway Rye Bread

Serving: 4 loaves (16 slices each). | Prep: 30mins | Ready in:

Ingredients

- 4 packages (1/4 ounce each) active dry yeast
- 4 cups warm water (110° to 115°)
- 1 cup warm milk (110° to 115°)
- 6 tablespoons brown sugar
- 1/4 cup sugar
- 1/4 cup shortening
- 1/4 cup molasses
- 2 tablespoons salt
- 2 cups rye flour
- 10 to 11 cups all-purpose flour
- 1/4 cup caraway seeds

Direction

- Dissolve yeast and warm water in a big bowl. Add in salt, molasses, shortening, sugars, and the milk. Add in 4 cups of all-purpose flour and rye flour, then whisk until smooth. Whisk in an enough amount of the remaining all-purpose flour and the caraway seeds to create soft dough.
- Transfer onto a floured surface and knead for about 6-8 minutes until elastic and smooth. Put into a very big bowl greased with cooking spray, or divide into 2 big bowls greased with cooking spray, flipping one time to grease top. Cover and allow rising for about an hour in a warm place until doubled.
- Punch the dough down. Transfer onto a lightly floured surface and divide into fourths. Form into 4 loaves. Arrange each loaf in a 9x5-inch loaf pan greased with cooking spray. Cover and allow rising for about half an hour until doubled.
- Bake for 30-35 minutes at 375° until golden brown. Transfer from pans to wire racks to cool.

Nutrition Information

- Calories: 105 calories
- Protein: 3g protein. Diabetic Exchanges: 1-1/2 starch.
- Total Fat: 1g fat (0 saturated fat)
- Sodium: 225mg sodium
- Fiber: 1g fiber)
- Total Carbohydrate: 21g carbohydrate (3g sugars
- Cholesterol: 1mg cholesterol

92. Graham Streusel Coffee Cake

Serving: 24 | Prep: | Ready in:

Ingredients

- 1 1/3 cups graham cracker crumbs
- 3/4 cup chopped walnuts
- 3/4 cup packed brown sugar
- 1 1/2 teaspoons ground cinnamon
- 2/3 cup butter, melted
- 1 (18.25 ounce) package yellow cake mix
- 1 cup water
- 1/4 cup vegetable oil
- 3 eggs
- 1 cup confectioners' sugar
- 1 1/2 teaspoons vanilla extract
- 1/2 teaspoon butter flavored extract (optional)

Direction

- Preheat an oven to 175 °C or 350 °F. Oil a pan, 9x13-inch in size. Prepare streusel: mix cinnamon, brown sugar, nuts and graham cracker crumbs in a medium size bowl. Mix in liquified butter. Reserve.
- Mix eggs, oil, water and cake mix in a big mixing bowl. Using electric mixer, whip on low speed barely till dampened. Whip for additional 2 minutes on moderate speed. In an oiled pan of 9x13-inch in size, scatter half of batter. Scatter on half of streusel mixture. On top of streusel, cautiously scatter the leftover half of cake batter, and scatter with the rest of streusel.
- Bake for 35 minutes to 40 minutes or till a toothpick pricked gets out clean. Cool partially, then sprinkle with powdered sugar icing. Serve while warm for best taste. Yield 12 or up to 16 servings.
- To prepare icing: Mix butter flavoring, vanilla and confectioners' sugar in small bowl. Put in several drops of water till you attain pourable consistency.

Nutrition Information

- Calories: 258 calories;
- Sodium: 217
- Total Carbohydrate: 32.8
- Cholesterol: 37
- Protein: 2.7
- Total Fat: 13.4

93. Grandma's Zwieback Rolls

Serving: 24 rolls. | Prep: 30mins | Ready in:

Ingredients

- 1 package (1/4 ounce) active dry yeast
- 1 teaspoon sugar
- 1/2 cup warm water (110° to 115°)
- 6 to 6-1/2 cups all-purpose flour, divided
- 1 tablespoon salt
- 3/4 cup butter, melted and cooled
- 2 cups scalded milk, cooked

Direction

- Melt sugar and yeast in water; put aside. Beat yeast mixture, milk, shortening, salt and 3 cups flour well in a big bowl. Add enough leftover flour to make a soft dough. Turn on lightly floured surface and knead for 6-8 minutes till elastic and smooth; it should be soft. Put dough into lightly greased bowl with cover and rise for 1 hour till doubled in a warm place. Punch down dough then divide to 4 pieces. Divide 3 pieces to 8 pieces each, forming to smooth balls. Put onto greased baking sheets. Divide leftover dough to 24 balls. Over each bigger ball, press 1 small ball; cover. Rise for 45 minutes till doubled then bake till golden for 30 minutes at 375°.
- Cooking for 2 option: In freezer containers/heavy-duty freezer bags, freeze baked rolls; when ready to serve, thaw.

Nutrition Information

- Calories: 168 calories
- Total Carbohydrate: 27g carbohydrate (0 sugars
- Cholesterol: 0 cholesterol
- Protein: 4g protein. Diabetic Exchanges: 2 starch
- Total Fat: 6g fat (0 saturated fat)
- Sodium: 299mg sodium
- Fiber: 0 fiber)

94. Hearty Graham Streusel Coffee Cake

Serving: 12-16 servings. | Prep: 20mins | Ready in:

Ingredients

- STREUSEL:
- 1-1/2 cups graham cracker crumbs
- 1 cup packed brown sugar
- 3/4 cup chopped pecans
- 2/3 cup butter, melted
- 2 teaspoons ground cinnamon
- CAKE:
- 1 package white cake mix with pudding (regular size)
- 3 large eggs, lightly beaten
- 1 cup water
- 1/4 cup canola oil

Direction

- Mix streusel ingredients in a big bowl; put aside. Beat oil, water, eggs and cake mix on low speed till mixed in another big bowl; beat for 2 minutes on medium speed. Put 1/2 in a 13x9-in. greased pan; sprinkle 1/2 streusel over. Spread leftover batter on streusel carefully; put leftover streusel on top.
- Bake for 35-40 minutes at 350° till an inserted toothpick in the middle of cake exits clean.

Nutrition Information

- Calories: 372 calories
- Protein: 4g protein.
- Total Fat: 20g fat (7g saturated fat)
- Sodium: 347mg sodium
- Fiber: 1g fiber)
- Total Carbohydrate: 46g carbohydrate (29g sugars
- Cholesterol: 60mg cholesterol

95. Hearty Mushroom Canapes

Serving: 2 servings. | Prep: 15mins | Ready in:

Ingredients

- 1/4 cup chopped fresh mushrooms
- 1/4 cup shredded Monterey Jack cheese
- 1/4 cup mayonnaise
- 6 slices caraway rye bread
- 1-1/2 teaspoons grated Parmesan cheese

Direction

- Mix the first 3 ingredients together in a small mixing bowl until well combined. Toast bread lightly; cut a heart out of each bread slice with a 3-inch heart-shaped cutter while bread is still warm. Spoon mushroom mixture onto bread and scatter Parmesan cheese over.
- Arrange on a baking sheet. Bake for 15 to 20 minutes at 350° until cheese is bubbly. Serve right away.

Nutrition Information

- Calories:
- Protein:
- Total Fat:
- Sodium:
- Fiber:
- Total Carbohydrate:
- Cholesterol:

96. Herb Biscuit Loaf

Serving: 8-10 servings. | Prep: 15mins | Ready in:

Ingredients

- 1/4 cup butter, melted
- 1/2 teaspoon dried minced onion
- 1/2 teaspoon dried basil
- 1/4 to 1/2 teaspoon caraway seeds
- 1/8 teaspoon garlic powder
- 2 tubes (12 ounces each) buttermilk biscuits

Direction

- Mix the first 5 ingredients together in a shallow bowl. Dip into butter mixture with biscuits, then fold in half and put in a 9-inch square baking pan coated with grease in rows.

Use leftover butter mixture to drizzle over, then bake at 350 degrees until turn golden brown, about 27 to 30 minutes.

Nutrition Information

- Calories: 123 calories
- Protein: 3g protein.
- Total Fat: 5g fat (3g saturated fat)
- Sodium: 337mg sodium
- Fiber: 0 fiber)
- Total Carbohydrate: 16g carbohydrate (0 sugars
- Cholesterol: 12mg cholesterol

97. Herb Potato Rolls

Serving: 2 dozen. | Prep: 30mins | Ready in:

Ingredients

- 5 to 5-1/2 cups all-purpose flour
- 1 cup mashed potato flakes
- 2 packages (1/4 ounce each) active dry yeast
- 1 tablespoon sugar
- 1 tablespoon minced chives
- 2 teaspoons salt
- 2 teaspoons minced fresh parsley
- 2 cups 2% milk
- 1/2 cup sour cream
- 2 eggs

Direction

- Mix together the parsley, salt, chives, sugar, yeast, potato flakes and 3 cups flour in a big bowl. Heat the sour cream and milk in a small saucepan to 120-130 degrees, then add it to the dry ingredients. Beat it for 2 minutes on medium speed. Add 1/2 cup flour and eggs and beat it for 2 minutes more. Mix in enough leftover flour until a soft dough forms.
- Flip it onto a floured surface and knead it for about 6 to 8 minutes, until it becomes pliable and smooth. Put it in a greased bowl and flip it once to grease the top. Put cover and allow it to rise for about 45 minutes in a warm area, until it doubles.
- Punch down the dough. Flip it onto a lightly floured surface and split it into 24 pieces. Form each into a roll. Put it in a greased 13x9-inch baking pan. Put cover and allow it to rise for around 35 minutes, until it doubles.
- Let it bake for 30 to 35 minutes at 375 degrees or until it turns golden brown in color. Transfer to wire racks.

Nutrition Information

- Calories: 137 calories
- Total Carbohydrate: 24g carbohydrate (2g sugars
- Cholesterol: 24mg cholesterol
- Protein: 5g protein. Diabetic Exchanges: 1-1/2 reduced-fat milk.
- Total Fat: 2g fat (1g saturated fat)
- Sodium: 221mg sodium
- Fiber: 1g fiber)

98. Herbed Brussels Sprouts

Serving: 8 servings. | Prep: 20mins | Ready in:

Ingredients

- 8 cups fresh Brussels sprouts (about 2-1/2 pounds)
- 1 cup sliced fresh mushrooms
- 1/4 cup packed brown sugar
- 1/4 cup cider vinegar
- 2 tablespoons butter, melted
- 1/2 teaspoon salt
- 1/2 teaspoon dried tarragon
- 1/2 teaspoon dried marjoram
- 1/2 teaspoon pepper
- 1/4 cup chopped pimientos

Direction

- Preheat the oven to 350°F. After trimming the Brussels sprouts, slice 'X' into the core of every one. Insert the sprouts into steamer basket then put the basket into a big saucepan with a little more than an inch of water in it. Lead to boiling point, steaming with the cover on until they become tender and crispy or for around 9 to 11 minutes. Use cooking spray to coat a 13 by 9 inches baking dish then put the sprouts on top of it. Add mushrooms over the top. Mix pepper, marjoram, tarragon, salt, butter, vinegar and brown sugar together in a small bowl then empty this mixture out atop the vegetables. Scatter pimientos atop. Bake without any cover on until they tenderize or for 15 to 20 minutes.

Nutrition Information

- Calories: 94 calories
- Cholesterol: 8mg cholesterol
- Protein: 3g protein. Diabetic Exchanges: 2 vegetable
- Total Fat: 3g fat (2g saturated fat)
- Sodium: 203mg sodium
- Fiber: 4g fiber)
- Total Carbohydrate: 16g carbohydrate (9g sugars

99. Holiday German Stollen

Serving: 3 loaves (12 slices each). | Prep: 30mins | Ready in:

Ingredients

- 8-1/2 to 9 cups all-purpose flour
- 1 cup plus 2 tablespoons sugar divided
- 2 packages (1/4 ounce each) active dry yeast
- 2 teaspoons salt
- 2 cups milk
- 1-3/4 cups butter, softened, divided
- 4 large eggs
- 1-1/2 teaspoons almond extract
- 1 teaspoon grated lemon peel
- 1 teaspoon rum extract, optional
- 1-1/2 cups slivered almonds
- 1 cup each red candied cherries, candied lemon peel and candied orange peel
- 1 cup raisins
- GLAZE:
- 1 cup confectioners' sugar
- 1/4 teaspoon vanilla extract
- 2 to 3 tablespoons milk

Direction

- Mix salt, yeast, 1 cup sugar and 3 cups flour in a big bowl. Heat 1 1/2 cups butter and milk to 120-130° in a saucepan. Add to dry ingredients and beat till just moist; beat in eggs till smooth. Mix in enough leftover flour to make soft dough. Add rum extract (optional), lemon peel and almond extract; mix in raisins, orange peel, candied lemon, cherries and almonds (dough will be a bit sticky).
- Turn onto heavily floured surface and knead for 6-8 minutes till elastic and smooth. Put into greased bowl; turn once to grease the top. Cover; allow to rise for 1 1/2 hours till nearly doubled in a warm place.
- Punch down dough; turn onto lightly floured surface and divide into thirds. Roll every portion to 15x8-in. oval. Melt leftover butter; brush 1 tbsp. butter on each oval. Sprinkle 2 tsp. leftover sugar. To within 1/2-in. from opposite side, fold long side of oval; lightly press edges to seal. Put in lightly greased/parchment-lined baking sheets; lightly curve ends. Cover; allow to rise for 30 minutes.
- Bake till golden brown for 30-35 minutes at 350°; brush with the leftover melted butter. Transfer from pans onto wire racks; cool. Mix glaze ingredients; drizzle on stollen.

Nutrition Information

- Calories: 327 calories
- Total Fat: 12g fat (6g saturated fat)
- Sodium: 263mg sodium

- Fiber: 2g fiber)
- Total Carbohydrate: 49g carbohydrate (24g sugars
- Cholesterol: 49mg cholesterol
- Protein: 6g protein.

100. Homemade Caraway Rye Bread

Serving: 2 loaves (16 slices each). | Prep: 25mins | Ready in:

Ingredients

- 2 packages (1/4 ounce each) active dry yeast
- 1-1/2 cups warm water (110° to 115°)
- 2/3 cup honey
- 3 tablespoons butter, softened
- 1 tablespoon caraway seeds
- 1 tablespoon finely grated carrot
- 1 teaspoon salt
- 2-3/4 cups rye flour
- 2 to 3 cups all-purpose flour
- Melted butter

Direction

- Dissolve yeast in a big bowl with warm water. Put in 1 cup of all-purpose flour, rye flour, salt, carrot, caraway seeds, butter and honey, then beat the mixture until smooth. Stir in enough amount of leftover all-purpose flour to make a soft dough.
- Turn dough out on a surface coated with flour and knead for 6 to 8 minutes, until elastic and smooth. Put dough into a bowl coated with grease and turn one time to grease top. Place a cover and allow to rise in a warm area for 1 1/4 hours, until doubled.
- Punch dough down then turn out on a surface coated lightly with flour and split into 2 equal portions. Form into loaves and put in 2 8"x4" loaf pans coated with grease. Place a cover and allow to rise for 45 minutes, until doubled.
- Bake at 350 degrees until turn golden brown, about 40 to 50 minutes. Allow to cool about 10 minutes prior to transferring from pans to wire racks. Use melted butter to brush over surface, then allow to cool.

Nutrition Information

- Calories: 92 calories
- Total Fat: 1g fat (1g saturated fat)
- Sodium: 86mg sodium
- Fiber: 2g fiber)
- Total Carbohydrate: 19g carbohydrate (6g sugars
- Cholesterol: 3mg cholesterol
- Protein: 2g protein.

101. Homemade Coleslaw Dressing

Serving: 6-8 servings. | Prep: 25mins | Ready in:

Ingredients

- 2 tablespoons sugar
- 1/2 teaspoon salt
- 1/4 teaspoon ground mustard
- 1/4 teaspoon paprika
- 4 egg yolks
- 1/2 cup water
- 1/3 cup white vinegar
- 2 cups shredded green cabbage
- 2 cups shredded red cabbage

Direction

- Whisk together egg yolks, paprika, mustard, salt and sugar in a heavy saucepan until smooth. Whisk in vinegar and water gradually, then cook and stir on moderate heat until mixture thickens and a thermometer reaches 160 degrees. Take away from the heat and allow to cool to room temperature.

- Put in a bowl with cabbage, then put in dressing and toss to coat well. Chill until ready to serve.

Nutrition Information

- Calories: 51 calories
- Sodium: 156mg sodium
- Fiber: 1g fiber)
- Total Carbohydrate: 5g carbohydrate (4g sugars
- Cholesterol: 106mg cholesterol
- Protein: 2g protein.
- Total Fat: 3g fat (1g saturated fat)

102. Homemade Croutons

Serving: Makes 1 cup | Prep: | Ready in:

Ingredients

- 3 slices stale firm-textured white bread
- 1 tablespoon or more softened unsalted butter, or 1 1/2 tablespoons extra-virgin olive oil
- 1/4 teaspoon crushed garlic (optional)

Direction

- Set the oven to 300°F.
- Trim and get rid of the bread's crusts.
- Butter both sides of each slice lightly (or, if you want, mix butter with crushed garlic first). I frequently replace butter with fruity extra-virgin olive oil, sometimes mixed with 1/4 tsp. crushed garlic, sometimes plain. One and a half tbsp. of oil is quite right because bread absorbs more oil than softened butter.
- Cut each buttered slice into 1/3-in. cubes and arrange on an ungreased big baking sheet in single layer and not touching each other.
- Place on the center oven shelf and toast for 15 minutes until pale tan.
- Use croutons as the recipe directs.

Nutrition Information

103. Homemade Rye Rolls

Serving: 20 rolls. | Prep: 40mins | Ready in:

Ingredients

- 2 cups rye flour
- 1/4 cup sugar
- 2 packages (1/4 ounce each) active dry yeast
- 1 tablespoon salt
- 2 to 3 teaspoons fennel seed
- 2 teaspoons caraway seeds
- 3-1/2 to 4-1/2 cups all-purpose flour
- 2-1/2 cups water
- 3 tablespoons shortening

Direction

- Mix 2 cups all-purpose flour, caraway seeds, fennel seed, salt, yeast, sugar and rye flour in a large bowl. Heat shortening and water to 120° to 130° in a saucepan. Put into the dry ingredients and beat just until moistened. Then beat for 3 minutes on medium speed. Mix in enough of the leftover flour to make a firm dough. Transfer to a floured surface and then knead for about 6 to 8 minutes until elastic and smooth. Put into a greased bowl and flip once to coat the top. Cover the dough and allow to rise in a warm place for about 1 hour until doubled.
- Punch the dough down and transfer to a lightly floured surface. Separate into 6 portions. Divide each piece into ten pieces and form each piece into a ball. Put 3 balls into each greased muffin cup. Cover the cups and allow to rise for about 30 minutes until doubled. Bake for 15 to 20 minutes at 375° or until turned golden brown. Cool for five minutes before transferring from the pans onto wire racks.

Nutrition Information

- Calories: 145 calories
- Total Carbohydrate: 28g carbohydrate (3g sugars
- Cholesterol: 0 cholesterol
- Protein: 4g protein. Diabetic Exchanges: 1-1/2 starch
- Total Fat: 2g fat (1g saturated fat)
- Sodium: 355mg sodium
- Fiber: 2g fiber)

104. Homemade Whole Wheat Pasta

Serving: 12 servings. | Prep: 45mins | Ready in:

Ingredients

- 4 cups all-purpose flour
- 1/2 cup whole wheat flour
- 2-1/4 teaspoons salt, divided
- 4 large eggs
- 1/2 cup plus 4 quarts water, divided
- 2 tablespoons olive oil
- 3 tablespoons butter
- 1/2 teaspoon pepper

Direction

- Combine 2 teaspoons salt and the flours in a large bowl. Make a hole in the center. Next, whisk the eggs, oil, and 1/2 cup water; pour into the hole. Stir together to form a dough. Cover and allow to rest for 10 minutes.
- Place the dough on a floured surface and knead for 8-10 times. Divide into 4 parts, then roll each into a 14x12-in. rectangle. Cut the widthwise into 1/2-in. strips and cut into 6-in. length strips. Allow the noodles to rest for at least 60 minutes on a clean towel.
- Boil the leftover water rapidly in a Dutch oven. Add noodles and cook until tender, for about 8-10 minutes. Strain.
- Cook the butter over medium heat until golden brown, for 3-4 minutes in the same pan. Add the leftover salt, pepper, and noodles; toss to coat.

Nutrition Information

- Calories: 162 calories
- Total Carbohydrate: 23g carbohydrate (1g sugars
- Cholesterol: 53mg cholesterol
- Protein: 5g protein. Diabetic Exchanges: 1-1/2 starch
- Total Fat: 6g fat (2g saturated fat)
- Sodium: 341mg sodium
- Fiber: 1g fiber)

105. Honey Mustard Green Beans

Serving: 2 servings. | Prep: 10mins | Ready in:

Ingredients

- 1/2 pound fresh green beans, trimmed
- 1 teaspoon cider vinegar
- 1 teaspoon olive oil
- 1 teaspoon Dijon mustard
- 1 teaspoon honey
- 1/8 teaspoon salt

Direction

- In a small saucepan, add beans and water to cover, then bring to a boil. Cover and cook until crisp-tender, about 4 to 7 minutes.
- At the same time, mix together salt, honey, mustard, oil and vinegar in a small bowl. Drain beans then put into vinegar mixture and toss to coat.

Nutrition Information

- Calories: 65 calories

- Protein: 2g protein. Diabetic Exchanges: 1 vegetable
- Total Fat: 2g fat (0 saturated fat)
- Sodium: 214mg sodium
- Fiber: 3g fiber)
- Total Carbohydrate: 11g carbohydrate (6g sugars
- Cholesterol: 0 cholesterol

106. Honey Mustard Sprouts

Serving: 2 servings. | Prep: 5mins | Ready in:

Ingredients

- 10 fresh or frozen brussels sprouts, halved
- 1-1/2 teaspoons butter, melted
- 1-1/2 teaspoons honey
- 1/2 teaspoon Dijon mustard
- Dash each onion powder and dill weed

Direction

- Cut X into the core of every Brussels sprouts after trimming it then insert it into a steamer basket. In a saucepan with an inch of water, insert the steamer basket and lead it to boiling point. Leave it cooking, covered up, for 8 to 12 minutes until the content becomes tender and just crispy. Make sure to drain thoroughly. Mix dill, onion powder, mustard, honey and butter together in a small bowl. Finish off by drizzling this mixture atop the sprouts. Coat everything by tossing.

Nutrition Information

- Calories: 125 calories
- Sodium: 109mg sodium
- Fiber: 7g fiber)
- Total Carbohydrate: 22g carbohydrate (0 sugars
- Cholesterol: 8mg cholesterol
- Protein: 7g protein. Diabetic Exchanges: 2 vegetable
- Total Fat: 4g fat (2g saturated fat)

107. Horseradish Dijon Potatoes

Serving: 4 servings. | Prep: 10mins | Ready in:

Ingredients

- 1-1/4 pounds red potatoes (about 5 medium), sliced
- 1/2 cup sour cream
- 4-1/2 teaspoons minced chives
- 3-1/2 teaspoons prepared horseradish
- 1 tablespoon minced fresh parsley
- 1 teaspoon lemon juice
- 1/2 teaspoon Dijon mustard
- 1/4 teaspoon salt
- 1/8 teaspoon pepper
- Lettuce leaves, optional

Direction

- In a big saucepan, add potatoes and water to cover, then bring to a boil. Lower heat and cook with a cover until softened, about 12 to 15 minutes. In the meantime, mix together pepper, salt, mustard, lemon juice, parsley, horseradish, chives and sour cream.
- Drain potatoes and allow to cool a bit. Put in dressing and stir gently to coat. Serve in a bowl lined with lettuce if you want.

Nutrition Information

- Calories: 166 calories
- Cholesterol: 20mg cholesterol
- Protein: 4g protein. Diabetic Exchanges: 1-1/2 starch
- Total Fat: 5g fat (4g saturated fat)
- Sodium: 195mg sodium
- Fiber: 3g fiber)

- Total Carbohydrate: 24g carbohydrate (3g sugars

108. Kaiserschmarren

Serving: 4 | Prep: 10mins | Ready in:

Ingredients

- 4 eggs, separated
- 1/2 cup milk
- 1/2 cup white sugar
- 1 pinch salt
- 1 cup all-purpose flour
- 2/3 cup raisins (optional)
- 1 tablespoon butter
- 2 tablespoons confectioners' sugar
- 2 cups applesauce (optional)

Direction

- In a clean bowl, beat egg whites until forming soft peaks. Lift your whisk or beater upward: egg whites will form soft mounds rather than a sharp peak. In another bowl, beat egg yolks until smooth; stir in raisins, flour, salt, sugar, and milk until just moist. Fold in beaten egg whites.
- Melt butter over medium heat in a large skillet. Transfer batter to the skillet and cook until golden brown; turn over and cook for about 1 minute until the other side is set. Use 2 forks to tear kaiserschmarren into pieces; keep cooking for about 2 more minutes or until golden brown. Scatter top with confectioners' sugar and drizzle with applesauce.

Nutrition Information

- Calories: 472 calories;
- Sodium: 109
- Total Carbohydrate: 89.9
- Cholesterol: 196
- Protein: 11.6
- Total Fat: 8.9

109. Knoephla Soup

Serving: 10 | Prep: 15mins | Ready in:

Ingredients

- Soup:
- 1/2 cup butter, cut into cubes
- 3 baking potatoes, peeled and cut into cubes
- 1 small onion, diced
- 1 1/2 teaspoons ground black pepper
- 3 cups whole milk
- 6 cups water
- 2 tablespoons chicken bouillon
- Knoephla:
- 1 1/2 cups all-purpose flour
- 7 tablespoons whole milk, or more as needed
- 1 egg, beaten
- 2 teaspoons dill weed
- 2 teaspoons parsley
- 1 teaspoon ground black pepper
- 1/2 teaspoon salt

Direction

- In the big skillet, melt the butter on medium heat; sauté one and a half tsp. of black pepper, onion and potatoes for roughly 20 minutes or till just softened. Mix 3 cups of milk into the potato mixture and heat for roughly 5 minutes or till nearly boiling. Take the skillet off from heat.
- In heavy pot or Dutch oven, boil chicken bouillon and water.
- In a bowl, mix together salt, 1 tsp. of pepper, parsley, dill, egg, 7 tbsp. of milk and flour till dough is stiff. If necessary, pour in extra milk, 1 tbsp. at a time. Roll the dough into ropes roughly half an inch in thickness on a working surface. Chop the ropes into a quarter-in. pieces and drop into the boiling broth. Lower the heat, cover the Dutch oven with a lid, and

let it simmer for roughly 10 minutes or till knoephla start to float.

- Mix the potato mixture into knoephla and broth; let simmer for roughly 20 minutes or till potatoes are soft.

Nutrition Information

- Calories: 264 calories;
- Cholesterol: 52
- Protein: 7
- Total Fat: 12.9
- Sodium: 457
- Total Carbohydrate: 30.7

110. Kolaches

Serving: 2 dozen. | Prep: 45mins | Ready in:

Ingredients

- 3 packages (1/4 ounce each) active dry yeast
- 1/2 cup warm water (110° to 115°)
- 1/2 cup sugar
- 1 package (3.4 ounces) instant vanilla pudding mix
- 1 cup (8 ounces) sour cream
- 1/2 cup vegetable oil
- 1 teaspoon salt
- 4 eggs
- 4-1/2 to 5 cups all-purpose flour
- 1 can (12 ounces) apricot, poppy seed or prune filling

Direction

- Dissolve yeast in a big bowl with water. Put in 2 cups of flour, eggs, salt, oil, sour cream, pudding mix and sugar, then beat the mixture until smooth. Stir in enough quantity of flour to make a soft dough then cover and chill dough overnight.
- Punch dough down. Turn dough out on a surface coated lightly with flour, then shape into 24 pieces. Form each piece into a ball, then arrange on baking sheets coated with grease, spaced 2 inches apart. Place a cover and allow to rise in a warm area for a half hour, until doubled.
- Use the end of a wooden spoon handle to create in the center of each ball with a big indentation, then fill in 2 tbsp. of filling. Bake about 14 to 15 minutes at 350 degrees, until browned slightly. Transfer from pans to wire racks to cool.

Nutrition Information

- Calories: 222 calories
- Protein: 4g protein.
- Total Fat: 7g fat (2g saturated fat)
- Sodium: 181mg sodium
- Fiber: 1g fiber)
- Total Carbohydrate: 34g carbohydrate (12g sugars
- Cholesterol: 42mg cholesterol

111. Lemon Dilled Brussels Sprouts

Serving: 4-6 servings. | Prep: 5mins | Ready in:

Ingredients

- 1-1/2 pounds fresh brussels sprouts
- 1/3 cup butter
- 2 tablespoons lemon juice
- 1 teaspoon dill weed
- 1/2 teaspoon salt
- 1/8 teaspoon pepper
- 2 tablespoons finely chopped walnuts

Direction

- Insert an inch of water and Brussels sprouts into the big saucepan then lead the mixture to boiling point. Lower the heat. Leave it simmering with a cover on until the sprouts tenderize, about 8 to 10 minutes. Meanwhile, put butter into a separate big saucepan and heat until melted. Add pepper, salt, dill and lemon juice, cooking and stirring for 60 seconds. After draining the sprouts, put them into the butter mixture. Coat everything by tossing. Finish off by scattering walnuts over the top.

Nutrition Information

- Calories: 117 calories
- Total Carbohydrate: 8g carbohydrate (2g sugars
- Cholesterol: 20mg cholesterol
- Protein: 3g protein.
- Total Fat: 9g fat (5g saturated fat)
- Sodium: 246mg sodium
- Fiber: 3g fiber)

112. Lemon/Raspberry Streusel Muffins

Serving: about 1 dozen. | Prep: 15mins | Ready in:

Ingredients

- 2 cups all-purpose flour
- 1/2 cup sugar
- 2 teaspoons baking powder
- 1/2 teaspoon baking soda
- 1/2 teaspoon salt
- 2 large eggs, lightly beaten
- 1 cup (8 ounces) lemon yogurt
- 1/2 cup vegetable oil
- 1 teaspoon grated lemon zest
- 1 cup fresh or frozen raspberries
- TOPPING:
- 1/3 cup sugar
- 1/4 cup all-purpose flour
- 2 tablespoons butter or margarine

Direction

- Mix together salt, sugar, baking powder, baking soda and flour in a large bowl. Mix together the eggs, yogurt, oil and lemon zest; combine thoroughly. Stir this mixture into the dry mix till everything is just moistened. Fold raspberries into the mix. Fill into muffin cups lined with paper or greased up to 3/4 full. To make topping, mix together the sugar and flour. Cut butter into the mix till it has coarse crumbs' texture; sprinkle about 1 tablespoon of the mixture on top of each muffin. Bake until muffins test done, at 400° for about 18-20 minutes. Let it cool down in pan for 10 minutes then take out to a wire rack.

Nutrition Information

- Calories: 272 calories
- Fiber: 1g fiber)
- Total Carbohydrate: 37g carbohydrate (18g sugars
- Cholesterol: 41mg cholesterol
- Protein: 4g protein.
- Total Fat: 12g fat (3g saturated fat)
- Sodium: 258mg sodium

113. Lemony Brussels Sprouts

Serving: 6 servings. | Prep: 10mins | Ready in:

Ingredients

- 1-1/2 pounds fresh brussels sprouts (about 2-1/2 cups), trimmed
- 1 teaspoon lemon juice
- 1/8 teaspoon salt
- 1/8 teaspoon pepper
- 1/3 cup butter, cubed
- 2 garlic cloves, minced

Direction

- At the core of every Brussels sprout, slice an X then put in into the saucepan. Pour in an inch of water before leading the whole thing to boiling point. Lower the heat. Leave it simmering with a cover on for 10 to 12 minutes until they become tender and crispy then drain it. Add pepper, salt, lemon juice and sprouts into a big skillet, sautéing them in butter until the flavors combine, around 2 to 3 minutes. Insert the garlic and continue cooking for another minute.

Nutrition Information

- Calories: 51 calories
- Sodium: 78mg sodium
- Fiber: 4g fiber)
- Total Carbohydrate: 11g carbohydrate (3g sugars
- Cholesterol: 0 cholesterol
- Protein: 4g protein. Diabetic Exchanges: 2 vegetable.
- Total Fat: 0 fat (0 saturated fat)

114. Liberty Sauerkraut Salad

Serving: 8 servings. | Prep: 10mins | Ready in:

Ingredients

- 1 can (14 ounces) sauerkraut, rinsed and drained
- 1 medium green pepper, diced
- 1 cup diced celery
- 1 medium onion, diced
- 3/4 to 1 cup sugar
- 1/2 cup cider vinegar
- 1 jar (2 ounces) diced pimientos, drained

Direction

- Mix entire of ingredients together in a 1-quart serving bowl. Place a cover and chill overnight. Serve together with a slotted spoon.

Nutrition Information

- Calories: 100 calories
- Cholesterol: 0 cholesterol
- Protein: 1g protein.
- Total Fat: 0 fat (0 saturated fat)
- Sodium: 343mg sodium
- Fiber: 2g fiber)
- Total Carbohydrate: 25g carbohydrate (21g sugars

115. Marinated Brussels Sprouts

Serving: 2-1/2 cups. | Prep: 15mins | Ready in:

Ingredients

- 1 package (10 ounces) frozen brussels sprouts
- 1 cup Italian salad dressing
- 1 tablespoon finely chopped onion
- 1 garlic clove, minced
- 1/2 teaspoon dill weed

Direction

- Follow the instructions on the packaging to cook the Brussels sprouts before draining. Mix the rest of the ingredients together then empty it out on top of the sprouts. Coat everything by tossing. Keep it in the fridge with a cover on.

Nutrition Information

- Calories: 41 calories
- Protein: 2g protein. Diabetic Exchanges: 1-1/2 vegetable.
- Total Fat: 1g fat (0 saturated fat)
- Sodium: 470mg sodium
- Fiber: 0 fiber)
- Total Carbohydrate: 8g carbohydrate (0 sugars
- Cholesterol: 0 cholesterol

116. Meatless Stuffed Cabbage

Serving: 6 servings. | Prep: 45mins | Ready in:

Ingredients

- 1/2 cup uncooked brown rice
- 1 cup water
- 1 medium head cabbage
- 1 package (12 ounces) frozen vegetarian meat crumbles, thawed
- 1 large onion, chopped
- 1/2 teaspoon pepper
- 1 can (10-3/4 ounces) reduced-sodium condensed tomato soup, undiluted, divided
- 1 can (8 ounces) Italian tomato sauce, divided
- 1 can (14-1/2 ounces) Italian diced tomatoes, undrained

Direction

- Bring water and rice to a boil in a small pot. Cover, decrease heat, and simmer until tender, 25-30 minutes. In the meantime, put cabbage in boiling water and cook until the outer leaves pull easily away from head. Take 12 large leaves for rolls and set aside. Put the remaining cabbage in fridge and use for a different dish. Start preheating oven to 350 degrees. Mix cooked rice, onion, half the soup, meat crumbles, and pepper in a big bowl. Cut the thick veins out of each cabbage leaf, make a V-shaped cut. Put 1/3 cup of the rice mixture on each of the leaves; overlap the cut ends. Fold in the sides, starting from the cut end. Enclose the filling completely by rolling up. Put half the tomato sauce in a greased 13x9-in. pan. With the seam down, put the rolls in the pan. Mix remaining soup and tomato sauce with the tomatoes in a small bowl. Dump on rolls. Cover; bake until cabbage is tender and bubbling, 40-45 minutes.

Nutrition Information

- Calories: 232 calories
- Total Fat: 3g fat (0 saturated fat)
- Sodium: 1000mg sodium
- Fiber: 7g fiber)
- Total Carbohydrate: 37g carbohydrate (12g sugars
- Cholesterol: 0 cholesterol
- Protein: 15g protein. Diabetic Exchanges: 2 starch

117. Microwave Brussels Sprouts

Serving: 8 servings. | Prep: 20mins | Ready in:

Ingredients

- 1-1/2 pounds brussels sprouts
- 1/4 cup water
- 1/4 teaspoon celery salt
- Pinch pepper
- 1/2 cup shredded cheddar cheese
- 1/3 cup finely crushed cornflakes
- 1 tablespoon butter, melted

Direction

- In a dish that's safe for the microwave and is around 1 1/2 quart in size, pour in water then insert the Brussels sprouts. Scatter pepper and celery salt before microwaving with a cover on at a high setting for 6 to 8 minutes until the sprouts tenderize before draining. Every two minutes that passes during the process, stir and rotate 1/4 turn. Scatter cheese over the top before microwaving for another 30 to 60 seconds at a high setting. It's ready when the cheese starts melting. Mix butter and cornflakes then scatter this on the sprouts.

Nutrition Information

- Calories: 88 calories
- Protein: 5g protein.
- Total Fat: 4g fat (2g saturated fat)
- Sodium: 151mg sodium

- Fiber: 3g fiber)
- Total Carbohydrate: 11g carbohydrate (2g sugars
- Cholesterol: 11mg cholesterol

118. Mushroom Omelet

Serving: Makes 1 serving. | Prep: 5mins | Ready in:

Ingredients

- 1 tsp. olive oil
- 1/2 cup sliced fresh mushrooms
- 2 egg s, beaten
- 1/8 tsp. fresh ground black pepper
- 2 Tbsp. PHILADELPHIA Chive Onion 1/3 Less Fat than Cream Cheese

Direction

- In a small nonstick frying pan, heat oil over medium-high heat. Add mushrooms, stir and cook for 2 minutes.
- Add pepper and eggs, cook until the eggs nearly set, about 2-3 minutes, raising the edge using a spatula and tip the frying pan to let the raw egg run underneath. Once the omelet top sets but still slightly moist, put small spoonfuls of reduced-fat cream cheese on top.
- Loosen the omelet by slipping the spatula underneath and tiping the frying pan and carefully fold the omelet in half. Flip or slide the omelet onto a serving dish.

Nutrition Information

- Calories: 260
- Saturated Fat: 7 g
- Fiber: 1 g
- Protein: 16 g
- Total Fat: 20 g
- Sodium: 310 mg
- Sugar: 2 g
- Total Carbohydrate: 4 g
- Cholesterol: 445 mg

119. Mustard Cheese Spread

Serving: 2 cups. | Prep: 10mins | Ready in:

Ingredients

- 1 package (8 ounces) cream cheese, softened
- 1/2 cup butter, softened
- 1 medium onion, finely chopped
- 2 garlic cloves, minced
- 2 to 3 tablespoons prepared mustard
- 2 tablespoons paprika
- 1/4 teaspoon salt
- 1/8 teaspoon pepper
- 1 tablespoon caraway seeds

Direction

- Beat butter and cream cheese in a bowl until smooth. Put in pepper, salt, paprika, mustard, garlic and onion then spread in an 8-inches serving platter. Sprinkle on top with caraway seeds, then cover and chill until ready to serve.

Nutrition Information

- Calories: 109 calories
- Total Fat: 11g fat (7g saturated fat)
- Sodium: 158mg sodium
- Fiber: 1g fiber)
- Total Carbohydrate: 2g carbohydrate (1g sugars
- Cholesterol: 31mg cholesterol
- Protein: 2g protein.

120. No Yeast Stollen

Serving: 1 loaf. | Prep: 35mins | Ready in:

Ingredients

- 2 tablespoons chopped candied orange peel
- 2 tablespoons chopped candied lemon peel
- 4 teaspoons water
- 1 teaspoon rum extract
- 1/4 teaspoon almond extract
- 1/4 teaspoon vanilla extract
- 2-1/2 cups all-purpose flour
- 3/4 cup sugar
- 1/2 cup ground almonds
- 2 teaspoons baking powder
- 1/2 teaspoon salt
- 1/4 teaspoon ground mace
- 1/8 teaspoon ground cardamom
- 5 tablespoons cold butter, divided
- 1 cup (8 ounces) 4% cottage cheese
- 2 eggs, beaten
- 1/2 cup golden raisins
- 1/2 cup dried currants
- 2 teaspoons confectioners' sugar

Direction

- Mix together extracts, water and candied peel in a small bowl, then put aside. Mix together cardamom, mace, salt, baking powder, almonds, sugar and flour in a big bowl, then slice in 4 tbsp. of butter until the mixture looks like fine crumbs.
- Stir in candied peel mixture, currants, raisins, egg and cottage cheese, then shape into a ball. Turn the dough out on a surface coated with flour and knead for 5 times. Roll kneaded dough into an oval, 8x10-in. in size. Fold over with a long side, to within 1 inch of the opposite side, then seal by pressing edge slightly.
- Put on a baking sheet coated with grease with curve ends lightly. Melt leftover butter and coat the dough surface with melted butter. Bake about 45 to 50 minutes at 350 degrees, until turn golden brown. Allow to cool on a wire rack, then sprinkle with confectioners' sugar.

Nutrition Information

- Calories: 195 calories
- Total Carbohydrate: 32g carbohydrate (17g sugars
- Cholesterol: 34mg cholesterol
- Protein: 5g protein.
- Total Fat: 6g fat (3g saturated fat)
- Sodium: 195mg sodium
- Fiber: 1g fiber)

121. Noodles Romanoff

Serving: 9 | Prep: 20mins | Ready in:

Ingredients

- 2 (8 ounce) packages wide egg noodles
- 2 (8 ounce) packages cream cheese
- 2 cups sour cream
- 1/2 cup minced onion
- 1 tablespoon Worcestershire sauce
- 1 teaspoon garlic salt
- 1 dash hot pepper sauce
- 1/2 cup bread crumbs

Direction

- Set an oven to 175°C (350°F) and start preheating. Allow to grease one 2-quart casserole dish.
- Following the package instructions, cook the noodles. Use cold water to wash and let drain.
- In a food processor or a blender, blend the hot pepper sauce, garlic salt, Worcestershire sauce, onion, sour cream, and cream cheese. Process until smooth; add into cooked noodles and stir. Transfer into the prepared casserole dish.
- Put breadcrumbs on top, bake at 175°C (350°F) for 25 minutes.

Nutrition Information

- Calories: 503 calories;
- Sodium: 452
- Total Carbohydrate: 44.6

- Cholesterol: 119
- Protein: 13.3
- Total Fat: 30.6

122. Noodles Romanoff For Two

Serving: 2 servings. | Prep: 5mins | Ready in:

Ingredients

- 2 cups uncooked egg noodles
- 1/2 cup sour cream
- 2 tablespoons butter, softened
- 2 tablespoons shredded Parmesan cheese
- 1/2 teaspoon salt-free herb seasoning blend
- 1/4 teaspoon garlic powder
- Dash pepper
- 2 teaspoons minced chives

Direction

- Follow directions on package to cook noodles. In the meantime, mix pepper, sour cream, seasoning blend, butter, garlic powder, and Parmesan in a small bowl. Drain water from noodles and return to pot. Dump sour cream mixture on top and mix to coat; cook through. Sprinkle chives on top.

Nutrition Information

- Calories: 389 calories
- Cholesterol: 106mg cholesterol
- Protein: 9g protein.
- Total Fat: 24g fat (16g saturated fat)
- Sodium: 194mg sodium
- Fiber: 1g fiber)
- Total Carbohydrate: 30g carbohydrate (3g sugars

123. Noodles And Kraut

Serving: 3 servings. | Prep: 15mins | Ready in:

Ingredients

- 2 cups uncooked egg noodles
- 1/4 cup butter, cubed
- 1/4 cup chopped onion
- 1 cup sauerkraut, rinsed and well drained

Direction

- Cook noodles as directed on the package; drain off water.
- Melt butter in a small skillet. Sauté onion in melted butter until softened. Add sauerkraut and noodles; cook over medium heat, stirring, for 2 minutes. Lower the heat; simmer without a cover, stirring from time to time, for 10 to 15 minutes.

Nutrition Information

- Calories: 293 calories
- Fiber: 3g fiber)
- Total Carbohydrate: 30g carbohydrate (2g sugars
- Cholesterol: 72mg cholesterol
- Protein: 6g protein.
- Total Fat: 17g fat (10g saturated fat)
- Sodium: 429mg sodium

124. Nutty Brussels Sprouts

Serving: 4-6 servings. | Prep: 20mins | Ready in:

Ingredients

- 1 pound fresh or frozen brussels sprouts, thawed and halved
- 1 cup water
- 1/2 teaspoon salt
- 1/4 teaspoon pepper
- 3 tablespoons butter

- 1/4 cup chopped pecans

Direction

- Start by washing and trimming the Brussels sprouts. At the core of the sprouts, slice 'X' in order to let them cook faster. Pour in an inch of water into a big saucepan. Add Brussels sprouts and salt. Lead it to boiling point then lower the heat. Leave it cooking with the cover on until the sprouts turn crispy and tender, about 8 to 10 minutes. After draining, scatter pepper over the top. Put butter into a small skillet and warm it up a medium heat until it is melted and a nice golden brown. Insert the pecans, cooking until they turn a little brown or for 1 to 2 minutes. Insert the Brussels sprouts, tossing until coated.

Nutrition Information

- Calories: 117 calories
- Protein: 3g protein.
- Total Fat: 9g fat (4g saturated fat)
- Sodium: 273mg sodium
- Fiber: 3g fiber)
- Total Carbohydrate: 8g carbohydrate (2g sugars
- Cholesterol: 15mg cholesterol

125. Old Fashioned German Coffee Cake

Serving: 2 coffee cakes. | Prep: 25mins | Ready in:

Ingredients

- 1 tablespoon active dry yeast
- 1 tablespoon sugar
- 1/2 cup warm water (110° to 115°)
- 1/3 cup shortening
- 1/2 cup sugar
- 1 large egg, beaten
- 3-1/2 to 4 cups all-purpose flour, divided
- 1/2 cup warm whole milk (80°-90°)
- TOPPING:
- 1 cup all-purpose flour
- 1/2 cup packed brown sugar
- 1/2 cup sugar
- 1/4 cup shortening
- 2 teaspoons vanilla extract
- Pinch salt
- 2 cans (15-1/4 ounces each) sliced peaches, drained

Direction

- Dissolve 1 tbsp. sugar and yeast in water for cake; allow to stand for 5 minutes. Mix egg, sugar and shortening in a big bowl. Mix in yeast mixture, milk and 2 cups flour slowly; add leftover flour enough to make soft dough. Turn onto floured surface; knead for 6-8 minutes till elastic and smooth. Put into greased bowl; turn to grease the top. Cover; allow to rise for 1 hour till doubled in a warm place. Punch down dough; halve. Press each half in 11x7-in. greased baking pan then cover; allow to rise for 1 hour till doubled. Mix all topping ingredients but peaches; sprinkle on dough. Put peach slices on top; bake till golden brown for 25-30 minutes at 375°.

Nutrition Information

- Calories:
- Total Carbohydrate:
- Cholesterol:
- Protein:
- Total Fat:
- Sodium:
- Fiber:

126. Old World Dark Bread

Serving: 2 loaves. | Prep: 30mins | Ready in:

Ingredients

- 4 to 4-1/2 cups all-purpose flour
- 4 cups rye flour
- 2 cups All-Bran
- 2 packages (1/4 ounce each) active dry yeast
- 2 tablespoons instant coffee granules
- 1 tablespoon sugar
- 1 tablespoon salt
- 1 tablespoon caraway seeds
- 1 teaspoon fennel seed, crushed
- 1/2 teaspoon ground coriander
- 3 cups water, divided
- 1/2 cup molasses
- 1/4 cup butter, cubed
- 2 tablespoons cider vinegar
- 1 ounce unsweetened chocolate
- 1 tablespoon cornstarch

Direction

- Mix together the first ten ingredients in a big bowl. Heat chocolate, vinegar, butter, molasses and 2 1/2 cups of water in a saucepan until the mixture reaches 120 degrees to 130 degrees. Put into dry mixture and beat just until blended.
- Turn dough out on a surface coated with flour and knead for 6 to 8 minutes, until elastic and smooth. Put dough into a bowl coated with grease and turn one time to coat top. Place a cover and allow to rise in a warm area for an hour and a half, until doubled.
- Punch dough down and turn out on a surface coated lightly with flour. Split dough in 2 equal portions, then form each into a ball. Put on baking sheets coated with grease, then cover and allow to rise for a half hour, until doubled.
- Bake at 375 degrees until turn golden brown, about 50 to 55 minutes. Transfer from pans to wire racks to cool.
- Mix together leftover water and cornstarch in a small saucepan until smooth. Bring to a boil then cook and stir until thickened, about 1 to 2 minutes. Brush the mixture over bread.

Nutrition Information

- Calories: 147 calories
- Cholesterol: 0 cholesterol
- Protein: 4g protein.
- Total Fat: 2g fat (1g saturated fat)
- Sodium: 251mg sodium
- Fiber: 4g fiber)
- Total Carbohydrate: 29g carbohydrate (5g sugars

127. Old World Rye Bread

Serving: 2 loaves (12 slices each). | Prep: 25mins | Ready in:

Ingredients

- 2 packages (1/4 ounce each) active dry yeast
- 1-1/2 cups warm water (110° to 115°)
- 1/2 cup molasses
- 6 tablespoons butter, softened
- 2 cups rye flour
- 1/4 cup baking cocoa
- 2 tablespoons caraway seeds
- 2 teaspoons salt
- 3-1/2 to 4 cups all-purpose flour
- Cornmeal

Direction

- Dissolve the yeast in the warm water in a large bowl. Beat in two cups of all-purpose flour, salt, caraway seeds, cocoa, rye flour, butter and molasses until smooth. Mix in enough remaining all-purpose flour to make the stiff dough.
- Place the dough onto the floured surface; knead for 6 to 8 mins or until elastic and smooth. Transfer to a greased bowl, turning once to grease the top. Cover and allow to rise in the warm place for 1-1/2 hours or until doubled in size.
- Punch the dough down. Place the dough onto the lightly floured surface; cut into two halves. Fit each piece into a 10 in. long loaf. Grease 2 baking sheets and scatter with the cornmeal.

Put the loaves on the prepared pans. Allow to rise, covered, for 60 mins or until doubled.
- Bake for 35 to 40 mins at 350°, until the bread sounds hollow when tapped. Take out of pans and cool on the wire racks.

Nutrition Information

- Calories: 146 calories
- Protein: 3g protein.
- Total Fat: 3g fat (2g saturated fat)
- Sodium: 229mg sodium
- Fiber: 2g fiber)
- Total Carbohydrate: 26g carbohydrate (5g sugars
- Cholesterol: 8mg cholesterol

128. Overnight Swedish Rye Bread

Serving: 4 loaves. | Prep: 30mins | Ready in:

Ingredients

- 2 packages (1/4 ounce each) active dry yeast
- 1/2 cup warm water (110° to 115°)
- 1 teaspoon sugar
- 4 cups warm milk (110° to 115°)
- 1 cup molasses
- 1 cup packed brown sugar
- 1 cup canola oil
- 1 cup quick-cooking oats
- 2 tablespoons grated orange zest
- 1 tablespoon salt
- 1 teaspoon fennel seed
- 1 teaspoon aniseed
- 1 teaspoon caraway seeds
- 2 cups rye flour
- 11 to 12 cups all-purpose flour

Direction

- Dissolve yeast in a big bowl with water, then stir in sugar and allow to stand about 5 minutes. Put in 6 cups of all-purpose flour, rye flour, caraway, aniseed, fennel, salt, orange zest, oats, oil, brown sugar, molasses and milk. Put in enough amount of leftover all-purpose flour to make soft dough yet still sticky. Cover and allow dough to rise in a warm area overnight.
- Punch dough down. Turn dough out on a surface coated with flour and knead for 6 to 8 minutes, until elastic and smooth. Form dough into 4 loaves, then put in 9"x5" loaf pans coated with grease. Place a cover and allow to rise for an hour, until doubled.
- Bake at 350 degrees about 35 to 45 minutes. Transfer from pans to wire racks to cool.

Nutrition Information

- Calories: 161 calories
- Fiber: 1g fiber)
- Total Carbohydrate: 27g carbohydrate (8g sugars
- Cholesterol: 2mg cholesterol
- Protein: 3g protein.
- Total Fat: 4g fat (1g saturated fat)
- Sodium: 122mg sodium

129. Pecan Brussels Sprouts

Serving: 4 servings. | Prep: 10mins | Ready in:

Ingredients

- 12 ounces fresh or frozen brussels sprouts (about 3 cups)
- 3 tablespoons water
- 1 cup pecan halves
- 2 tablespoons butter, melted
- 1/4 teaspoon salt
- 1/8 teaspoon pepper
- 1/8 teaspoon ground nutmeg

Direction

- Cut Brussels sprouts and make an X in the middle of every sprout. Place Brussels sprouts in a microwavable safe dish with water; cover. Set the microwave on high for 3-4mins until the sprouts are tender. Drain the sprouts; toss in nutmeg, pecans, pepper, butter, and salt to coat.

Nutrition Information

- Calories: 274 calories
- Protein: 5g protein.
- Total Fat: 25g fat (5g saturated fat)
- Sodium: 227mg sodium
- Fiber: 6g fiber)
- Total Carbohydrate: 11g carbohydrate (3g sugars
- Cholesterol: 15mg cholesterol

130. Pennsylvania Dutch Coleslaw

Serving: 12-16 servings. | Prep: 15mins | Ready in:

Ingredients

- 1 medium head green cabbage, shredded (about 8 cups)
- 1 cup shredded red cabbage
- 4 to 5 carrots, shredded
- 1 cup mayonnaise
- 2 tablespoons cider vinegar
- 1/2 cup sugar
- 1 teaspoon salt
- 1/4 teaspoon pepper

Direction

- Mix carrots and cabbage together in a big bowl; set aside. Mix the remaining ingredients together in a small bowl; toss it with the cabbage mixture. Mix well and let it chill in the refrigerator overnight.

Nutrition Information

- Calories: 146 calories
- Fiber: 2g fiber)
- Total Carbohydrate: 11g carbohydrate (9g sugars
- Cholesterol: 5mg cholesterol
- Protein: 1g protein.
- Total Fat: 11g fat (2g saturated fat)
- Sodium: 239mg sodium

131. Plum Streusel Kuchen

Serving: 12-15 servings. | Prep: 25mins | Ready in:

Ingredients

- 2 cups all-purpose flour
- 1/4 cup sugar
- 2 teaspoons baking powder
- 2 tablespoons shortening
- 1 egg
- 1 cup heavy whipping cream
- 6 fresh plums, sliced
- TOPPING:
- 2/3 cup all-purpose flour
- 2/3 cup sugar
- 2 tablespoons cold butter
- 2 tablespoons heavy whipping cream

Direction

- Preheat an oven to 350°. Mix baking powder, sugar and flour in a big bowl; cut shortening into the mixture until fine crumbs are formed. Whisk cream and egg in another bowl, then add to crumb mixture; gently toss with a fork until it forms into a ball.
- Press dough into a 13x9-in. baking dish coated with cooking spray; put plums on crust.
- Topping: Mix sugar and flour in a small bowl; cut butter into the mixture until it fine crumbs are formed. Add cream; gently mix with a fork until moist crumbs appear. Sprinkle on plums.

- Bake until a toothpick slid into the middle gets out clean for 35-40 minutes; place on wire rack to cool.

Nutrition Information

- Calories: 237 calories
- Cholesterol: 43mg cholesterol
- Protein: 3g protein.
- Total Fat: 10g fat (6g saturated fat)
- Sodium: 80mg sodium
- Fiber: 1g fiber)
- Total Carbohydrate: 33g carbohydrate (15g sugars

132. Plum Topped Chocolate Kuchen

Serving: 12 servings. | Prep: 25mins | Ready in:

Ingredients

- 2 cups sliced fresh plums
- 1/4 cup port wine
- 1 tablespoon honey
- 1/2 cup butter, divided
- 5 tablespoons finely chopped hazelnuts, divided
- 2 ounces unsweetened chocolate, coarsely chopped
- 2 eggs
- 2/3 cup plus 3 tablespoons sugar, divided
- 2 tablespoons 2% milk
- 1-1/2 cups all-purpose flour
- 2 teaspoons baking powder
- 1/2 teaspoon salt
- 1/2 teaspoon baking soda
- 1/2 teaspoon ground cinnamon
- Whipped cream and confectioners' sugar, optional

Direction

- Mix honey, wine and plums in a small bowl; allow to stand for 30 minutes.
- Meanwhile, grease 1-in. up sides and bottom of the 9-in. springform pan using 1 tbsp. butter; top with 3 tbsp. hazelnuts. Put pan onto baking sheet; put aside.
- Preheat an oven to 375°. Melt leftover butter and chocolate in a microwave; mix till smooth. Cool it to room temperature. Mix milk, 2/3 cup sugar and eggs in a big bowl. Add chocolate mixture. Mix baking soda, salt, baking powder and flour; add to chocolate mixture slowly till just combined. Pour into prepped pan.
- Drain plums; keep 2 tbsp. liquid. Put plums on batter; drizzle with the reserved liquid. Mix leftover sugar and cinnamon and hazelnuts; sprinkle on top.
- Bake till inserted toothpick in middle exits clean for 35-40 minutes; cool for 10 minutes on wire rack. Run a knife around pan's edges to loosen carefully; serve cold/warm. If desired, garnish using confectioners' sugar and whipped cream.

Nutrition Information

- Calories: 263 calories
- Fiber: 2g fiber)
- Total Carbohydrate: 34g carbohydrate (19g sugars
- Cholesterol: 56mg cholesterol
- Protein: 4g protein.
- Total Fat: 13g fat (7g saturated fat)
- Sodium: 286mg sodium

133. Potato Stuffing Casserole

Serving: 6-8 servings. | Prep: 20mins | Ready in:

Ingredients

- 1/4 cup chopped celery
- 1 onion, chopped

- 4 tablespoons butter, divided
- 3 slices bread, cubed
- 4 to 5 large potatoes, peeled, cooked and mashed
- 1/4 cup chopped fresh parsley
- 1/2 teaspoon salt
- 1/4 teaspoon pepper
- 1 cup hot whole milk
- 1 large egg, beaten
- Additional parsley

Direction

- Saute onion and celery together in a medium skillet with 2 tbsp. of butter until soft. Put in bread cubes and stir until browned slightly. Stir in egg, milk, pepper, salt, parsley and potatoes, mixing well.
- Scoop into a 1 1/2-quart baking dish coated with grease, then dot with leftover butter. Bake at 350 degrees without a cover until browned slightly, about 30 to 40 minutes. Use more parsley to decorate.

Nutrition Information

- Calories: 258 calories
- Sodium: 295mg sodium
- Fiber: 4g fiber)
- Total Carbohydrate: 41g carbohydrate (6g sugars
- Cholesterol: 46mg cholesterol
- Protein: 7g protein.
- Total Fat: 8g fat (4g saturated fat)

134. Pronto Potato Pancakes

Serving: 8 pancakes. | Prep: 15mins | Ready in:

Ingredients

- 2 large eggs
- 1 small onion, halved
- 2 medium potatoes, peeled and cut into 1-inch cubes
- 2 to 4 tablespoons all-purpose flour
- 1/2 teaspoon salt
- 1/8 teaspoon cayenne pepper
- 4 to 6 tablespoons canola oil
- Applesauce, optional

Direction

- In a blender, add onion and eggs, then cover and process until combined. Put in potatoes, then cover and process until chopped finely. Turn to a small bowl, then stir in cayenne, salt and flour.
- In a big nonstick skillet, heat 2 tbsp. of oil on moderate heat. Drop into hot oil with batter by 1/4 cupfuls. Fry in batches, until both sides turn golden brown, using remaining oil as necessary. Drain on paper towels and serve together with apple sauce, if wanted.

Nutrition Information

- Calories: 263 calories
- Protein: 6g protein.
- Total Fat: 17g fat (2g saturated fat)
- Sodium: 338mg sodium
- Fiber: 3g fiber)
- Total Carbohydrate: 23g carbohydrate (2g sugars
- Cholesterol: 93mg cholesterol

135. Pumpernickel Bread

Serving: 1 loaf (2-1/4 pounds, 12 slices). | Prep: 20mins | Ready in:

Ingredients

- 1 cup warm water (70° to 80°)
- 1 cup warm buttermilk (70° to 80°)
- 3 tablespoons olive oil
- 4-1/2 teaspoons molasses

- 1 teaspoon salt
- 3-1/2 cups rye flour
- 2/3 to 1 cup all-purpose flour
- 3 teaspoons active dry yeast

Direction

- Put all the ingredients in bread machine pan in the order recommended by machine's maker. Set the machine to the dough setting (after five minutes of mixing, check the dough and add one to two tablespoons of flour or water if necessary).
- Once the cycle has ended, turn the dough onto a surface that is lightly floured. Form into an 8-inch round loaf. Transfer onto a baking sheet that is greased. Cover the dough and allow to rise in a warm place for about half an hour until doubled.
- Bake for 40 to 45 minutes at 350 degrees or until you hear a hollow sound when you tap the bread. Transfer onto a wire rack to cool.

Nutrition Information

- Calories: 134 calories
- Sodium: 165mg sodium
- Fiber: 4g fiber)
- Total Carbohydrate: 24g carbohydrate (2g sugars
- Cholesterol: 1mg cholesterol
- Protein: 3g protein. Diabetic Exchanges: 1-1/2 starch
- Total Fat: 3g fat (0 saturated fat)

136. Pumpernickel Muffins

Serving: 6 muffins. | Prep: 20mins | Ready in:

Ingredients

- 3/4 cup rye flour
- 2/3 cup all-purpose flour
- 3 tablespoons sugar
- 1 teaspoon baking powder
- 1/2 teaspoon ground cinnamon
- 1/4 teaspoon baking soda
- 1/4 teaspoon salt
- 1 egg
- 2/3 cup buttermilk
- 1/4 cup canola oil
- 1 tablespoon molasses
- 1/2 ounce unsweetened chocolate, melted and cooled
- 1/4 cup dried cherries

Direction

- Mix together salt, baking soda, cinnamon, baking powder, sugar and flours in a big bowl.
- Mix together chocolate, molasses, oil, buttermilk and egg in another bowl, then stir into dry mixture just until blended. Fold in cherries.
- Fill dough into muffin cups coated with grease or lined with paper until 3/4 full. Bake at 400 degrees until a toothpick exits clean after being inserted in the muffin, about 15 to 20 minutes. Allow to cool about 5 minutes prior to transferring from pan to a wire rack. Serve warm.

Nutrition Information

- Calories: 264 calories
- Total Fat: 12g fat (2g saturated fat)
- Sodium: 260mg sodium
- Fiber: 3g fiber)
- Total Carbohydrate: 36g carbohydrate (13g sugars
- Cholesterol: 36mg cholesterol
- Protein: 5g protein.

137. Pumpkin Gingerbread Bundt Coffee Cake

Serving: 16 servings. | Prep: 15mins | Ready in:

Ingredients

- 2 eggs
- 1/2 cup egg substitute
- 1 can (15 ounces) solid-pack pumpkin
- 1-1/2 cups honey
- 1/2 cup butter, melted
- 1/2 cup fat-free plain yogurt
- 1 cup toasted wheat germ
- 3 cups all-purpose flour
- 2 teaspoons baking soda
- 2 teaspoons ground ginger
- 1 teaspoon ground cinnamon
- 1 teaspoon ground nutmeg
- 1/2 teaspoon salt
- 1/4 teaspoon ground cloves
- ICING:
- 3/4 cup confectioners' sugar
- 2 teaspoons fat-free milk
- 1/4 teaspoon vanilla extract

Direction

- Beat egg substitute and eggs in big bowl; mix yogurt, butter, honey and pumpkin in till smooth. Mix wheat germ in. Mix dry ingredients; add to pumpkin mixture slowly. Stir well. Use cooking spray to coat 10-in. fluted tube pan; dust using flour then add batter.
- Bake for 55-60 minutes at 350° till an inserted toothpick in middle exits clean. Cool for 10 minutes; remove from pan onto wire rack to completely cool. Mix icing ingredients till smooth; drizzle on top of cake.

Nutrition Information

- Calories: 299 calories
- Cholesterol: 42mg cholesterol
- Protein: 6g protein.
- Total Fat: 7g fat (4g saturated fat)
- Sodium: 319mg sodium
- Fiber: 3g fiber)
- Total Carbohydrate: 55g carbohydrate (0 sugars

138. Quicker Stollen

Serving: 1 loaf. | Prep: 20mins | Ready in:

Ingredients

- 1 package (16 ounces) hot roll mix
- 1/4 cup sugar
- 1 cup warm water (120° to 130°)
- 2 tablespoons butter
- 1 large egg, beaten
- 3/4 teaspoon grated lemon zest
- 1/4 teaspoon almond extract
- 1/3 cup raisins
- 1/4 cup mixed candied fruit
- 1/4 cup chopped almonds
- GLAZE:
- 3/4 cup confectioners' sugar
- 1 to 2 tablespoons whole milk
- Additional candied cherries and sliced almonds, optional

Direction

- Mix sugar and contents of yeast packets and roll mix in a bowl; mix in extract, lemon zest, egg, butter and water to make a soft dough. Turn onto a floured surface; knead in almonds, candied fruit and raisins for about 5 minutes. Cover; rest for 5 minutes.
- Press/roll the dough out to a 12x7-in. oval. Fold a long side over to within 1" of its opposite side; lightly press the edge to enclose. Put onto a greased baking sheet; slightly curve ends. Cover; allow to rise for about 20-30 minutes until almost doubled.
- Bake at 375 degrees until golden brown, 20 minutes; place on wire rack to cool. Mix milk and confectioners' sugar; spread onto stollen. If desired, garnish with almonds and cherries.

Nutrition Information

- Calories: 251 calories
- Sodium: 283mg sodium

- Fiber: 2g fiber)
- Total Carbohydrate: 46g carbohydrate (20g sugars
- Cholesterol: 23mg cholesterol
- Protein: 5g protein.
- Total Fat: 5g fat (1g saturated fat)

139. Radish Dip

Serving: 16 | Prep: 10mins | Ready in:

Ingredients

- 4 cloves garlic, peeled
- 6 radishes, quartered
- 2 (8 ounce) packages cream cheese, softened

Direction

- Add garlic and pulse till finely minced in a food processor container. Add radishes; mince. Add the cream cheese; mix till blended well. Put onto a serving dish; chill till serving.

Nutrition Information

- Calories: 99 calories;
- Total Carbohydrate: 1.1
- Cholesterol: 31
- Protein: 2.2
- Total Fat: 9.8
- Sodium: 84

140. Raisin Walnut Dark Rye Bread

Serving: 1 loaf (1-1/2 pounds, 12 slices). | Prep: 15mins | Ready in:

Ingredients

- 3/4 cup water (70° to 80°)
- 1/4 cup molasses
- 1 tablespoon butter
- 2 tablespoons baking cocoa
- 1 tablespoon caraway seeds
- 1 teaspoon salt
- 1-1/4 cups bread flour
- 1 cup rye flour
- 1 tablespoon quick-rise yeast
- 1 teaspoon cornmeal
- 1/2 cup golden raisins
- 1/2 cup chopped walnuts, toasted

Direction

- Measure the first nine ingredients in the pan of bread machine in order manufacturer recommended. Choose dough setting. After 5 minutes of mixing, check dough; if needed, add 1-2 tablespoons flour or water.
- Take a baking sheet to grease and then sprinkle cornmeal. Turn dough onto a lightly floured surface as cycle is completed. Knead in walnuts and raisins. Round the loaf; remove to prepared pan. Cover with a kitchen towel; let rise in a warm environment, about 45 minutes or until it doubles in size. Prepare the oven to 375deg.
- Bring to bake until dark golden brown, about 30-35 minutes. Transfer to a wire rack to let it rest.

Nutrition Information

- Calories:
- Protein:
- Total Fat:
- Sodium:
- Fiber:
- Total Carbohydrate:
- Cholesterol:

141. Raisin Gingerbread Muffins

Serving: About 1 dozen. | Prep: 10mins | Ready in:

Ingredients

- 1/2 cup butter, softened
- 1/2 cup sugar
- 2 eggs
- 1/2 cup sour cream
- 1/2 cup molasses
- 2 cups plus 1 tablespoon all-purpose flour, divided
- 1 teaspoon baking soda
- 1 teaspoon ground ginger
- 1/4 teaspoon ground allspice
- 1/4 teaspoon ground cinnamon
- 1/2 cup golden raisins

Direction

- Cream the sugar and butter in a big bowl. Add in eggs, 1 egg at a time and beat well after each addition. Whisk in the molasses and sour cream. Mix the cinnamon, allspice, ginger, baking soda, and 2 cups of flour and pour into the creamed mixture until just moistened. Toss the remaining flour with the raisins and whisk into the batter.
- Line the muffin cups with paper and fill them 3/4 full. Bake for 18-20 minutes at 375° until the toothpick comes out clean. Let it cool for 5 minutes then take away from pans and move to wire racks.

Nutrition Information

- Calories: 265 calories
- Protein: 4g protein.
- Total Fat: 10g fat (6g saturated fat)
- Sodium: 204mg sodium
- Fiber: 1g fiber)
- Total Carbohydrate: 40g carbohydrate (21g sugars
- Cholesterol: 63mg cholesterol

142. Raisin Rye Bread

Serving: Makes 2 Loaves | Prep: | Ready in:

Ingredients

- 2 cups milk
- 1/2 cup warm water (105°F. to 115°F.)
- 1/2 cup packed golden brown sugar
- 2 envelopes dry yeast
- 1/2 cup plus 1 tablespoon unsulfured (light) molasses
- 1/2 cup vegetable oil
- 2 teaspoons grated orange peel
- 1 1/2 teaspoons salt
- 2 1/2 cups rye flour*
- 1/2 cup old-fashioned oats
- 1 teaspoon caraway seeds, crushed
- 1/2 teaspoon fennel seeds, crushed
- 1/2 teaspoon aniseed, crushed
- 5 cups (about) bread flour
- 1 cup raisins
- *Rye flour is sold at natural foods stores, specialty foods stores and some supermarkets.

Direction

- Preparation: In a small saucepan, heat milk to simmer. Let cool to between 105°F and 115°F. Combine sugar and warm water in a large bowl until sugar is dissolved. Scatter yeast over. Allow to stand for about 8 minutes until foamy. Stir in salt, orange peel, oil, 1/2 cup of molasses, and milk. Add aniseed, fennel seeds, caraway seeds, oats, and rye flour, then stir until well-combined. Mix in 2 cups of bread flour. Let rest, with a cover, for 15 minutes.
- Slowly mix in enough the leftover bread flour to make the dough. Turn out the dough onto a floured surface. Knead for about 12 minutes until elastic and smooth, putting in additional flour if sticky. Knead in raisins. Grease a large bowl with oil. Put in the dough, turning to coat. Use a clean kitchen towel to cover the bowl. In a warm spot, let rise for about 1 hour until doubled.

- Grease two 9-inch-diameter cake pans with oil. Line parchment on the bottom of the pans. Grease the parchment with oil. Cover pans and parchment with flour; shake to remove the excess. Punch the down dough. Turn out onto a lightly greased surface. Separate the dough into 2 portions. Form each into a 6-inch round loaf. Place loaves into prepared pans; press slightly. Use a clean kitchen towel to cover. Allow to rise in a warm spot for about 45 minutes until almost doubled and loaves seem spread nearly to edges of pans.
- Start preheating the oven to 350°F. Bake loaves until a tester comes out clean when inserted into the center, about 45 minutes or less. Let loaves cool in pans on racks for 5 minutes. Take loaves out of pans. Brush 1 tablespoon of molasses on tops. Let cool fully on racks. (Can be prepared 1 day beforehand. Wrap tightly; reserve at room temperature.)

Nutrition Information

- Calories: 352
- Fiber: 4 g(14%)
- Total Carbohydrate: 63 g(21%)
- Cholesterol: 3 mg(1%)
- Protein: 8 g(16%)
- Total Fat: 8 g(13%)
- Saturated Fat: 1 g(5%)
- Sodium: 214 mg(9%)

143. Red Cabbage Apple Slaw

Serving: 2 servings. | Prep: 15mins | Ready in:

Ingredients

- 3/4 cup diced peeled tart apple
- 1 tablespoon lemon juice
- 1-3/4 cups shredded red cabbage
- 2 tablespoons mayonnaise
- 2 tablespoons plain yogurt
- Dash each onion salt, white pepper and celery seed

Direction

- Start tossing lemon juice with apple in a bowl then mix in the rest of the ingredients. Coat everything by tossing. Serve at once.

Nutrition Information

- Calories: 152 calories
- Fiber: 2g fiber)
- Total Carbohydrate: 11g carbohydrate (9g sugars
- Cholesterol: 7mg cholesterol
- Protein: 1g protein.
- Total Fat: 12g fat (2g saturated fat)
- Sodium: 145mg sodium

144. Red Cabbage Casserole

Serving: 8-10 servings. | Prep: 10mins | Ready in:

Ingredients

- 8 cups shredded red cabbage
- 1 medium onion, chopped
- 1/4 cup sugar
- 1 tablespoon canola oil
- 1 teaspoon salt
- 1 teaspoon lemon juice
- 1 to 2 medium tart apples, chopped
- 1/4 cup red currant jelly

Direction

- Mix the first 6 ingredients in a Dutch oven, then place a cover and cook until cabbage is tender yet still crispy while stirring sometimes, about 10 to 15 minutes.
- Put in apples, then cook until apples and cabbage are both softened, about 10 to 15 minutes. Stir in jelly until melted.

Nutrition Information

- Calories: 80 calories
- Sodium: 243mg sodium
- Fiber: 2g fiber)
- Total Carbohydrate: 17g carbohydrate (15g sugars
- Cholesterol: 0 cholesterol
- Protein: 1g protein.
- Total Fat: 1g fat (0 saturated fat)

145. Red Cabbage Slaw

Serving: 6 | Prep: 15mins | Ready in:

Ingredients

- 1 small head red cabbage, thinly sliced and chopped
- 1/2 cup grated carrot
- 1/2 cup mayonnaise
- 1/4 cup dried cranberries
- 1/4 cup chopped walnuts
- 1 tablespoon milk, or more as needed
- 1 tablespoon apple cider vinegar
- 1 teaspoon white sugar, or more to taste

Direction

- In a bowl, mix together the cabbage, cranberries, carrot, walnuts, cider vinegar, milk, mayonnaise and sugar. Mix to coat well, then chill, covered, for about 4 hours.

Nutrition Information

- Calories: 216 calories;
- Total Fat: 18
- Sodium: 137
- Total Carbohydrate: 14.1
- Cholesterol: 7
- Protein: 2.4

146. Red Cabbage With Cranberries

Serving: 8 servings. | Prep: 10mins | Ready in:

Ingredients

- 1 tablespoon olive oil
- 1/2 cup packed brown sugar, divided
- 8 garlic cloves, minced
- 3 cups fresh or frozen cranberries, divided
- 1/2 cup red wine vinegar
- 1 medium head red cabbage, shredded (10 cups)
- 1 cup dry red wine or apple juice
- 1/2 teaspoon salt
- 1/8 to 1/4 teaspoon cayenne pepper

Direction

- In a kettle or Dutch oven, over medium heat, heat 1/4 cup of brown sugar and oil. Add in garlic, sauté 2 minutes. Mix in vinegar and 2 cups cranberries. Put on cover and cook on medium heat till berries are popped, or 3-4 minutes.
- Add wine (or apple juice) and cabbage; cook 15 minutes with cover on medium heat, mixing from time to time, or until cabbage is tender. Mix in brown sugar, the rest of cranberries, cayenne, and salt. Take away from heat. Put on cover and let sit till the berries are tender, or about 5 minutes.

Nutrition Information

- Calories: 142 calories
- Total Fat: 2g fat (0 saturated fat)
- Sodium: 167mg sodium
- Fiber: 4g fiber)
- Total Carbohydrate: 27g carbohydrate (21g sugars
- Cholesterol: 0 cholesterol
- Protein: 2g protein.

147. Rich Fruit Kuchens

Serving: 4 coffee cakes (8 servings each). | Prep: 40mins | Ready in:

Ingredients

- 1 1/8 teaspoons active dry yeast
- 1/2 cup warm water (110° to 115°)
- 1/2 cup warm milk (110° to 115°)
- 1/2 cup sugar
- 1/2 teaspoon salt
- 1/2 cup canola oil
- 1 large egg, lightly beaten
- 3-1/2 cups all-purpose flour, divided
- CUSTARD:
- 4 large eggs, lightly beaten
- 2 cups heavy whipping cream
- 1-1/2 cups sugar
- 8 to 10 cups sliced peeled tart apples or canned sliced peaches, drained, or combination of fruits
- TOPPING:
- 1/2 cup sugar
- 1/2 cup all-purpose flour
- 1 teaspoon ground cinnamon
- 1/4 cup cold butter

Direction

- Dissolve yeast in warm water in a big bowl. Add 2 1/2 cups flour, egg, oil, salt, sugar and milk; beat until smoothened. Mix in enough leftover flour to make a soft dough. Put into a greased bowl; turn once to grease the top. Don't knead. Cover; refrigerate overnight.
- To make custard: The next day, whisk sugar, cream and eggs until incorporated in a big bowl; put aside. Divide the dough into 4 portions.
- Roll every portion into a 10-in. circle on a lightly floured surface; press every circle down the bottom and up the sides of a dry 9-in. pie plate. In each crust, put 2-2 1/2 cups of fruit; pour 1 cup of custard onto the fruit.
- To make topping: In a small bowl, mix cinnamon, flour and sugar; cut in butter until coarse crumbs are formed. On each coffee cake, sprinkle 1/3 cup over; use foil to cover dough edges. Bake for 35-40 minutes at 350° until custard achieves 160° and golden brown.

Nutrition Information

- Calories: 242 calories
- Sodium: 69mg sodium
- Fiber: 1g fiber)
- Total Carbohydrate: 32g carbohydrate (19g sugars
- Cholesterol: 58mg cholesterol
- Protein: 3g protein.
- Total Fat: 11g fat (5g saturated fat)

148. Rich And Creamy Brussels Sprouts

Serving: 6-8 servings. | Prep: 5mins | Ready in:

Ingredients

- 1-1/4 pounds fresh brussels sprouts or 1 package (18 ounces) frozen brussels sprouts
- 1 can (10-3/4 ounces) condensed cream of mushroom soup, undiluted
- 1/4 cup whole milk
- 1 cup shredded sharp cheddar cheese
- 1/8 teaspoon salt
- 1/8 teaspoon pepper
- 1 can (8 ounces) sliced water chestnuts, drained
- 1/2 cup slivered almonds, toasted

Direction

- In a pot of boiling water, insert the sprouts and leave it cooking. Mix pepper, salt, cheese, milk and soup in a saucepan and leave it cooking at medium heat. Continue stirring until the cheese starts melting. After draining the sprouts, move it into a serving dish. Insert cheese sauce and water chestnuts and finish off by scattering almonds atop. Serve at once.

Nutrition Information

- Calories: 169 calories
- Total Fat: 10g fat (4g saturated fat)
- Sodium: 413mg sodium
- Fiber: 5g fiber)
- Total Carbohydrate: 15g carbohydrate (3g sugars
- Cholesterol: 18mg cholesterol
- Protein: 8g protein.

149. Roasted Autumn Vegetables

Serving: Makes 10 servings | Prep: | Ready in:

Ingredients

- Nonstick vegetable oil spray
- 1 1/2 pounds butternut squash, peeled, cut into 3x1/2-inch wedges
- 1 1/2 pounds rutabagas, peeled, cut into 1/2-inch-thick wedges
- 1 1/4 pounds red-skinned sweet potatoes (yams), cut into 2x3/4-inch wedges
- 2 tablespoons olive oil
- 1/4 teaspoon cayenne pepper
- 1/2 cup finely chopped red onion
- 1/4 cup chopped fresh chives
- 2 tablespoons apple cider vinegar

Direction

- Preheat the oven to 350°F. Use non-stick spray to coat a big rimmed baking sheet. In a big bowl, mix sweet potatoes, rutabagas and squash together. Insert cayenne and oil, tossing until coated. Scatter pepper and salt over the top. On prepped baking sheet, distribute the vegetable mixture. For around 60 minutes, leave them roasting until the vegetables tenderize. During the process, flip it over and stir from time to time. (The veggies can be prepped four hours in advance, just leave it standing at room temperate on a baking sheet. Warm it up again for around 15 minutes at 350°F in the oven until thoroughly heated.) Move the vegetable mixture in a bowl then insert vinegar, chives and red onion, tossing to combine. Add pepper and salt to season.

Nutrition Information

- Calories: 158
- Saturated Fat: 1 g(3%)
- Sodium: 43 mg(2%)
- Fiber: 5 g(19%)
- Total Carbohydrate: 26 g(9%)
- Protein: 2 g(5%)
- Total Fat: 6 g(9%)

150. Roasted Brussels Sprouts

Serving: 6 | Prep: 15mins | Ready in:

Ingredients

- 1 1/2 pounds Brussels sprouts, ends trimmed and yellow leaves removed
- 3 tablespoons olive oil
- 1 teaspoon kosher salt
- 1/2 teaspoon freshly ground black pepper

Direction

- Set the oven to 400 deg F.
- In a large air-tight plastic container, add olive oil, kosher salt, and pepper together with trimmed Brussels sprouts. Cover tight and shake to mix thoroughly. Place on a baking sheet and set on the center oven rack.
- Cook for 30 to 45 minutes inside the oven, In 5 to 7 minute intervals, shake the pan to brown the sides evenly and adjust the heat as needed to avoid burning. If the Brussels sprouts

appear dark brown to almost black, they are done. Remove from oven and add salt to taste. Serve right away.

Nutrition Information

- Calories: 104 calories;
- Sodium: 344
- Total Carbohydrate: 10
- Cholesterol: 0
- Protein: 2.9
- Total Fat: 7.3

151. Roasted Vegetables

Serving: 12 | Prep: 15mins | Ready in:

Ingredients

- 1 small butternut squash, cubed
- 2 red bell peppers, seeded and diced
- 1 sweet potato, peeled and cubed
- 3 Yukon Gold potatoes, cubed
- 1 red onion, quartered
- 1 tablespoon chopped fresh thyme
- 2 tablespoons chopped fresh rosemary
- 1/4 cup olive oil
- 2 tablespoons balsamic vinegar
- salt and freshly ground black pepper

Direction

- Preheat an oven to 245 degrees C (475 degrees F).
- Mix Yukon Gold potatoes, squash, sweet potato, and red bell peppers in a large bowl. Divide red onion quarters into pieces and place them into the mixture.
- Mix together pepper, salt, vinegar, thyme, rosemary, and olive oil in a small bowl. Mix with the vegetables until they're coated. Arrange evenly onto a large roasting pan.
- Roast for about 35 to 40 minutes while stirring every 10 minutes or until the vegetables are browned and cooked through.

Nutrition Information

- Calories: 123 calories;
- Total Fat: 4.7
- Sodium: 13
- Total Carbohydrate: 20
- Cholesterol: 0
- Protein: 2

152. Root Vegetables

Serving: 16-18 servings. | Prep: 15mins | Ready in:

Ingredients

- 2 cups pearl onions
- 2 pounds red potatoes, cut into 1/2-inch pieces
- 1 large rutabaga, peeled and cut into 1/2-inch pieces
- 1 pound parsnips, peeled and cut into 1/2-inch pieces
- 1 pound carrots, cut into 1/2-inch pieces
- 3 tablespoons butter, melted
- 3 tablespoons olive oil
- 4-1/2 teaspoons dried thyme
- 1-1/2 teaspoons salt
- 3/4 teaspoon coarsely ground pepper
- 2 packages (10 ounces each) frozen brussels sprouts, thawed
- 3 to 4 garlic cloves, minced

Direction

- Pour six cups of water into a big kettle or Dutch oven and lead it to boiling point. Insert the pearl onions and leave them boiling for three minutes. After draining, run them through cold water before peeling. Mix the carrots, parsnips, rutabaga, potatoes and onions together in a big roasting pan. Add oil and butter in a drizzling motion. Scatter pepper, salt and thyme. Coat everything by tossing. After putting a cover on, proceed with baking for 1/2-hour at 425°F. Remove the cover. Add garlic and Brussels sprouts, stirring. Continue baking without any cover on until the veggies start browning and tenderizing, around 50 to 60 minutes. During the process, stir from time to time.

Nutrition Information

- Calories:
- Sodium:
- Fiber:
- Total Carbohydrate:
- Cholesterol:
- Protein:
- Total Fat:

153. Rotkohl (Red Cabbage)

Serving: 7 servings. | Prep: 15mins | Ready in:

Ingredients

- 1/2 teaspoon whole peppercorns
- 2 bay leaves
- 2 whole cloves
- 2 medium onions, chopped
- 1/4 cup butter, cubed
- 1 garlic clove, minced
- 1 cup dry red wine or grape juice
- 1 medium head red cabbage, shredded
- 3 medium apples, chopped
- 1-1/2 teaspoons salt
- 1/4 teaspoon pepper
- 2 tablespoons red wine vinegar

Direction

- Onto a double thickness of cheesecloth, put cloves, bay leaves and peppercorns. Lift up the corners of the cloth and then tie using a string to make a bag.
- Sauté onions in butter in a Dutch oven until tender. Place in garlic and then cook for one minute. Pour in wine while stirring to loosen any browned bits from the pan. Add spice bag, pepper, salt, apples, and cabbage.
- Heat to boil. Lower the heat. Cover and let to simmer while stirring from time to time for about 30 to 35 minutes or until the cabbage is tender. Mix in vinegar. Get rid of spice bag. You can serve with a slotted spoon.

Nutrition Information

- Calories: 154 calories
- Sodium: 587mg sodium
- Fiber: 5g fiber)
- Total Carbohydrate: 22g carbohydrate (13g sugars
- Cholesterol: 17mg cholesterol
- Protein: 3g protein.
- Total Fat: 7g fat (4g saturated fat)

154. Ruby Slaw

Serving: 20-24 servings. | Prep: 15mins | Ready in:

Ingredients

- 1 medium head red cabbage (about 1-1/2 pounds)
- 1 medium head green cabbage (about 1-1/2 pounds)
- 5 tablespoons white vinegar, divided
- 1 medium onion, chopped
- 2 medium red apples, chopped
- 2 tablespoons brown sugar
- 1 tablespoon Dijon mustard
- 1/2 cup sour cream
- 1/2 cup mayonnaise
- 2 tablespoons crumbled blue cheese
- 1 tablespoon minced chives

- 1 tablespoon chopped fresh parsley or 1 teaspoon dried parsley flakes
- 1/2 teaspoon salt
- 1/2 teaspoon pepper

Direction

- Shred or chop the cabbage into thin slices and put it in an 8-quart Dutch oven. Put in 2 tablespoons of vinegar. Cover the Dutch oven and let it cook for 8-10 minutes over medium heat while stirring from time to time until the cabbage becomes tender and crispy. Add the remaining vinegar, onion, sugar, apples, and mustard. Let it cook without cover for 2-3 minutes.
- Transfer the cooked mixture in a big bowl; cover and keep it in the fridge for 1 hour until it is cold.
- Add the rest of the ingredients; stir until well-coated. Cover the mixture and keep it in the fridge for not less than 6 hours.

Nutrition Information

- Calories: 79 calories
- Sodium: 114mg sodium
- Fiber: 2g fiber)
- Total Carbohydrate: 8g carbohydrate (5g sugars
- Cholesterol: 6mg cholesterol
- Protein: 2g protein.
- Total Fat: 5g fat (1g saturated fat)

155. Rustic Apple Raisin Bread

Serving: 2 loaves (8 slices each). | Prep: 25mins | Ready in:

Ingredients

- 1 package (1/4 ounce) active dry yeast
- 1/4 cup warm water (110° to 115°)
- 1 cup unsweetened applesauce
- 1/2 cup warm fat-free milk (110° to 115°)
- 2 tablespoons sugar
- 2 tablespoons butter, softened
- 1 teaspoon salt
- 1 egg, separated
- 4 to 4-1/2 cups all-purpose flour
- 1 cup raisins
- 1 teaspoon caraway seeds
- 1 tablespoon cold water

Direction

- Dissolve yeast in a big bowl with warm water. Put in 2 cups of flour, egg yolk, salt, butter, sugar, milk and applesauce, then beat together until smooth. Stir in enough amount of leftover flour to make a firm dough, then stir in caraway seeds and raisins.
- On a surface coated lightly with flour, turn dough out and knead for 6 to 8 minutes, until elastic and smooth. Put in a bowl coated with grease and turn one time to grease top. Place a cover and allow to rise in a warm area for an hour, until doubled.
- Punch dough down. On a surface coated lightly with flour, turn out dough and split in two even portions. Form each into a ball and put on a baking sheet greased with cooking spray, spaced 4 inches apart. Pat into 6-inch round loaves, then cover and allow to rise for 45 minutes, until nearly doubled.
- Beat cold water and egg whites together in a small bowl, then brush over surface of loaves. Bake at 375 degrees until turn golden brown, about 30 to 35 minutes. Allow to cool on a wire rack.

Nutrition Information

- Calories: 175 calories
- Protein: 4g protein. Diabetic Exchanges: 2 starch
- Total Fat: 2g fat (1g saturated fat)
- Sodium: 172mg sodium
- Fiber: 2g fiber)

- Total Carbohydrate: 35g carbohydrate (10g sugars
- Cholesterol: 17mg cholesterol

156. Rye Biscuits

Serving: 4 biscuits. | Prep: 5mins | Ready in:

Ingredients

- 1/3 cup all-purpose flour
- 1/4 cup rye flour
- 1 tablespoon brown sugar
- 1 teaspoon baking powder
- 1/4 teaspoon caraway seeds
- 1/8 teaspoon salt
- 2 tablespoons cold butter
- 1 egg
- 1 tablespoon half-and-half cream

Direction

- Mix the first 6 ingredients in a small-sized bowl. Chop in butter till the mixture looks like coarse crumbs. Mix in cream and egg till just moistened.
- Drop batter into four mounds 2 inches apart onto the baking sheet that is coated using the cooking spray. Bake at 400 degrees till turning golden brown in color or for 10 to 12 minutes. Transfer to a wire rack right away. Serve while warm.

Nutrition Information

- Calories: 148 calories
- Sodium: 209mg sodium
- Fiber: 1g fiber)
- Total Carbohydrate: 17g carbohydrate (0 sugars
- Cholesterol: 70mg cholesterol
- Protein: 3g protein. Diabetic Exchanges: 1-1/2 fat
- Total Fat: 8g fat (4g saturated fat)

157. Rye Rolls

Serving: 2-1/2 dozen. | Prep: 40mins | Ready in:

Ingredients

- 1 tablespoon active dry yeast
- 2 cups warm water (110° to 115°)
- 4 eggs
- 1/2 cup nonfat dry milk powder
- 1/4 cup butter, softened
- 1/4 cup packed brown sugar
- 2 tablespoons dark molasses
- 2 teaspoons salt
- 1/2 teaspoon baking soda
- 3 to 4 cups all-purpose flour
- 3 cups rye flour
- 1 tablespoon cold water
- Caraway seeds and/or kosher salt

Direction

- In warm water, dissolve the yeast in a big bowl. Put in 2 cups all-purpose flour, baking soda, salt, molasses, brown sugar, butter, milk powder and 3 eggs. Mix till smooth. Put in rye flour and sufficient leftover all-purpose flour to make a soft dough; dough will become sticky.
- Transfer to a thoroughly floured area; knead for 6 to 8 minutes, till pliable and smooth. Put in a greased bowl, flipping one time to coat the surface. Put on cover and allow to rise in a warm area for an hour till doubled in size.
- Split the dough into 30 portions; form each into a round. Put on greased baking sheets, 2 inches apart.
- Beat the rest of the egg and the cold water in a small bowl; brush on top of dough. Scatter with kosher salt and/or caraway seeds. Put on cover and allow to rise for 45 minutes till doubled in size.

- Bake till golden brown, or about 14 to 16 minutes or at 350°. Transfer onto the wire racks.

Nutrition Information

- Calories: 123 calories
- Protein: 4g protein. Diabetic Exchanges: 1-1/2 starch.
- Total Fat: 3g fat (1g saturated fat)
- Sodium: 211mg sodium
- Fiber: 2g fiber)
- Total Carbohydrate: 21g carbohydrate (4g sugars
- Cholesterol: 33mg cholesterol

158. Santa Pancakes

Serving: 9 servings. | Prep: 30mins | Ready in:

Ingredients

- 2 cups biscuit/baking mix
- 1 teaspoon ground cinnamon
- 2 eggs, lightly beaten
- 1 cup milk
- 1 teaspoon vanilla extract
- 2 medium bananas, sliced
- 18 semisweet chocolate chips
- 1 can (21 ounces) cherry pie filling
- Whipped cream in a can

Direction

- Mix cinnamon with the baking mix in a big bowl. Combine vanilla, milk, and eggs in a small bowl, mix into the dry ingredients until just moistened.
- Put the batter on an oiled hot griddle, 1/4 cupfuls. Flip when bubbles start to show on the top, cook until the second side turns golden brown.
- On individual dishes, put the pancakes. Put 2 slices of banana on each pancake to make the Santa's eyes, put a chocolate chip on top. Slice the rest of the banana slices into two to make the ears, put on each side of the pancake. Use 9 cherries from the pie filling to make the nose, put one in the middle of the pancakes. Put 1/4 cup of the pie filling overhead the pancakes to make the hat. Spray pom-pom, hat brim, and the beard with whipped cream.

Nutrition Information

- Calories: 255 calories
- Total Fat: 7g fat (2g saturated fat)
- Sodium: 376mg sodium
- Fiber: 2g fiber)
- Total Carbohydrate: 44g carbohydrate (24g sugars
- Cholesterol: 51mg cholesterol
- Protein: 5g protein.

159. Santa's Surprise Gingerbread Muffins

Serving: 16 muffins. | Prep: 15mins | Ready in:

Ingredients

- 1/2 cup butter, softened
- 1/2 cup sugar
- 1/2 cup packed brown sugar
- 2 large eggs
- 1/2 cup molasses
- 3 cups all-purpose flour
- 1-1/2 teaspoons ground cinnamon
- 1 teaspoon baking soda
- 1/4 teaspoon each ground ginger, cloves and allspice
- 1 cup buttermilk
- 1/2 cup cranberry-raspberry sauce

Direction

- Cream sugars and butter together in a big bowl until fluffy and light. Put in 1 egg at a time while beating well between additions. Beat in molasses. Mix together allspice, cloves, ginger, baking soda, cinnamon and flour, then put into the creamed mixture together with buttermilk, alternately.

- Fill batter into sixteen muffin cups coated with grease or lined with paper until 1/2 full. Scoop over each cup with 1 1/2 tsp. of cranberry-raspberry sauce, then put leftover batter on top. Bake at 350 degrees until a toothpick exits clean after being inserted in the center, about 25 to 30 minutes. Allow to cool about 10 minutes prior to transferring from pans to wire racks to cool thoroughly.

Nutrition Information

- Calories: 244 calories
- Sodium: 170mg sodium
- Fiber: 1g fiber)
- Total Carbohydrate: 43g carbohydrate (24g sugars
- Cholesterol: 43mg cholesterol
- Protein: 4g protein.
- Total Fat: 7g fat (4g saturated fat)

160. Saucy Brussels Sprouts

Serving: 2 servings. | Prep: 10mins | Ready in:

Ingredients

- 1 package (10 ounces) frozen brussels sprouts
- 1 tablespoon finely chopped onion
- 1 tablespoon butter
- 2 teaspoons brown sugar
- 1 teaspoon all-purpose flour
- 1/4 teaspoon salt
- 1/4 teaspoon ground mustard
- Dash pepper
- 1/4 cup milk
- 1/4 cup sour cream
- 1 jar (2 ounces) diced pimientos, drained

Direction

- Cook Brussels sprouts following the package instructions. Meanwhile, sauté onion with butter in a big pot until tender; mix in pepper, brown sugar, mustard, flour, and salt until well combined. Slowly pour in milk; boil. Cook and stir for a minute; turn to low heat.
- Drain the Brussels sprouts then slice in half; toss in the sauce. Heat the mixture through; mix in pimientos and sour cream.

Nutrition Information

- Calories: 219 calories
- Protein: 8g protein.
- Total Fat: 12g fat (8g saturated fat)
- Sodium: 403mg sodium
- Fiber: 6g fiber)
- Total Carbohydrate: 21g carbohydrate (10g sugars
- Cholesterol: 39mg cholesterol

161. Sauerkraut Rye Bread

Serving: 12 | Prep: 10mins | Ready in:

Ingredients

- 1 cup sauerkraut - rinsed and drained
- 3/4 cup warm water
- 1 1/2 tablespoons molasses
- 1 1/2 tablespoons butter
- 1 1/2 tablespoons brown sugar
- 1 teaspoon caraway seed
- 1 1/2 teaspoons salt
- 1 cup rye flour
- 2 cups bread flour
- 1 1/2 teaspoons active dry yeast

Direction

- Follow the order of putting the ingredients into the bread machine pan suggested by the manufacturer. Choose the Basic Bread cycle on the machine and press the Start button to run the machine.

Nutrition Information

- Calories: 63 calories;
- Cholesterol: 4
- Protein: 1.1
- Total Fat: 1.6
- Sodium: 433
- Total Carbohydrate: 11.5

162. Sauerkraut Salad

Serving: 6 | Prep: | Ready in:

Ingredients

- 1 quart sauerkraut, drained
- 1 onion, chopped
- 2 stalks celery, chopped
- 1 green bell pepper, chopped
- 1 large carrots, chopped
- 1 (4 ounce) jar diced pimento peppers, drained
- 1 teaspoon mustard seed
- 1 1/2 cups white sugar
- 1 cup vegetable oil
- 1/2 cup cider vinegar

Direction

- Mix pimentos, mustard seed, celery, carrot, sauerkraut, green bell pepper, and onion in a large bowl; set aside.
- Boil sugar, vinegar, and oil in a small saucepan; boil Remove it from heat once done.
- Drizzle sugar mixture over the salad. Cover the bowl and store it inside the refrigerator for 2 days before serving.

Nutrition Information

- Calories: 577 calories;
- Total Fat: 37.2
- Sodium: 1057
- Total Carbohydrate: 62.2
- Cholesterol: 0
- Protein: 2.4

163. Sauerkraut Slaw

Serving: 6 servings. | Prep: 15mins | Ready in:

Ingredients

- 2 cans (14 ounces each) sauerkraut, rinsed and drained
- 2 cups chopped celery
- 1 cup chopped onion
- 1 jar (2 ounces) diced pimientos, drained
- 1 medium green pepper, chopped
- 1/2 cup julienned carrot
- 1-1/2 cups sugar
- 1/3 cup cider vinegar

Direction

- Mix pimientos, carrot, sauerkraut, onion, celery, and green pepper in a bowl. Mix vinegar and sugar in another bowl until the sugar has fully dissolved. Drizzle it on top of the vegetable mixture. Cover the bowl and keep it in the fridge for 8 hours or throughout the night.

Nutrition Information

- Calories: 235 calories
- Protein: 2g protein.
- Total Fat: 0 fat (0 saturated fat)
- Sodium: 479mg sodium
- Fiber: 4g fiber)
- Total Carbohydrate: 59g carbohydrate (52g sugars
- Cholesterol: 0 cholesterol

164. Sauteed Cabbage

Serving: 6 | Prep: 20mins | Ready in:

Ingredients

- 3 tablespoons olive oil
- 1/2 head red cabbage, chopped
- 1/2 onion, chopped
- 1 small red bell pepper, chopped
- 1 small yellow bell pepper, chopped
- salt and ground black pepper to taste

Direction

- In a big skillet, heat olive oil on high heat, then cook and stir in the hot oil the yellow bell pepper, red bell pepper, onion and cabbage for 5-7 minutes while stirring every half minute, until soft. Use pepper and salt to season.

Nutrition Information

- Calories: 96 calories;
- Total Fat: 6.9
- Sodium: 21
- Total Carbohydrate: 8.4
- Cholesterol: 0
- Protein: 1.5

165. Savory Bread

Serving: 2 loaves (9 slices each). | Prep: 25mins | Ready in:

Ingredients

- 1-1/2 cups water (70° to 80°)
- 2 tablespoons olive oil, divided
- 1/4 cup dried minced onion
- 2 teaspoons sugar
- 1-1/4 teaspoons salt
- 1 teaspoon dill weed
- 1/2 teaspoon onion powder
- 3-1/2 cups all-purpose flour
- 3/4 cup whole wheat flour
- 1 package (1/4 ounce) active dry yeast

Direction

- Add in a bread machine pan with yeast, flours, onion powder, dill, salt, sugar, minced onion, 1 tbsp. of oil and water, following manufacturer's suggested order. Choose the dough setting. Check dough after 5 minutes of mixing, then put in 1-2 tbsp. of flour or water if necessary.
- Once cycle is finished, turn dough out on a surface coated lightly with flour. Split dough in 2 even portions, then form each into a 7-inch round loaf. Arrange on baking sheets coated with grease, then place a cover and allow to rise for 40 minutes, until doubled.
- Bake about 15 to 20 minutes at 400 degrees, until turn golden brown. Use leftover oil to brush and transfer from pans to wire racks.

Nutrition Information

- Calories: 125 calories
- Cholesterol: 0 cholesterol
- Protein: 3g protein. Diabetic Exchanges: 1-1/2 starch.
- Total Fat: 2g fat (0 saturated fat)
- Sodium: 165mg sodium
- Fiber: 1g fiber)
- Total Carbohydrate: 24g carbohydrate (1g sugars

166. Savory Dill And Caraway Scones

Serving: 1 dozen. | Prep: 20mins | Ready in:

Ingredients

- 2 cups all-purpose flour
- 4-1/2 teaspoons sugar
- 1 tablespoon onion powder

- 1 tablespoon snipped fresh dill or 1 teaspoon dill weed
- 2 teaspoons caraway seeds
- 1 teaspoon baking powder
- 3/4 teaspoon salt
- 1/2 teaspoon baking soda
- 1/2 teaspoon coarsely ground pepper
- 6 tablespoons cold butter
- 1 large egg yolk
- 3/4 cup sour cream
- 1/2 cup ricotta cheese
- 4 teaspoons heavy whipping cream
- Additional caraway seeds, optional

Direction

- Mix initial 9 ingredients in a big bowl. Cut butter in till it looks like coarse crumbs. Mix ricotta cheese, sour cream and egg yolk; mix into crumb mixture till just moist. Turn onto floured surface then knead 10 times.
- Pat to 2 6-in. circles. Slice each to 6 wedges then separate wedges. Put on greased baking sheets. Brush cream on tops. If desired, sprinkle extra caraway seeds. Bake for 15-18 minutes till golden brown at 400°F then serve warm.

Nutrition Information

- Calories: 184 calories
- Sodium: 293mg sodium
- Fiber: 1g fiber)
- Total Carbohydrate: 18g carbohydrate (2g sugars
- Cholesterol: 49mg cholesterol
- Protein: 4g protein.
- Total Fat: 10g fat (7g saturated fat)

167. Simple Stollen

Serving: 1 loaf. | Prep: 25mins | Ready in:

Ingredients

- 2-1/4 cups all-purpose flour
- 1/2 cup sugar
- 1-1/2 teaspoons baking powder
- 1/4 teaspoon salt
- 7 tablespoons cold butter, divided
- 1 cup ricotta cheese
- 1/2 cup chopped mixed candied fruit
- 1/2 cup raisins
- 1/3 cup slivered almonds, toasted
- 1 teaspoon vanilla extract
- 1/2 teaspoon almond extract
- 1/2 teaspoon grated lemon peel
- 1 egg
- 1 egg yolk
- Confectioners' sugar

Direction

- Mix together salt, baking powder, sugar and flour in a big bowl. Slice in 6 tbsp. of butter until mixture looks like fine crumbs. Mix together yolk, egg, lemon peel, extracts, almonds, raisins, candied fruit and ricotta in a small bowl. Stir into flour mixture just until combined.
- Turn dough out on a surface coated with flour and knead for 5 times. Roll dough into an oval, 8x10-inch in size. Fold over with a long side to within 1 inch of opposite side, then seal by pinching edge slightly. Arrange on a baking sheet coated with grease with curve ends somewhat.
- Bake at 350 degrees until turn golden brown, about 40 to 45 minutes. Melt leftover butter and brush over loaf surface. Transfer to a wire rack to cool thoroughly, then sprinkle with confectioners' sugar.

Nutrition Information

- Calories: 284 calories
- Sodium: 209mg sodium
- Fiber: 2g fiber)
- Total Carbohydrate: 41g carbohydrate (20g sugars
- Cholesterol: 62mg cholesterol

- Protein: 6g protein.
- Total Fat: 11g fat (6g saturated fat)

168. Special Cauliflower

Serving: 3 servings. | Prep: 10mins | Ready in:

Ingredients

- 2 cups fresh caulifloweret s
- 1 tablespoon plain yogurt
- 1 tablespoon mayonnaise
- 1/2 teaspoon Dijon mustard
- 1/8 teaspoon dill weed
- 1/8 teaspoon salt
- 1/8 teaspoon garlic powder
- 1/4 cup shredded cheddar cheese

Direction

- In a steamer basket set in a small saucepan over 1 inch of water, add cauliflower and bring water to a boil. Place a cover and steam cauliflower until crisp-tender, about 6 to 8 minutes.
- In the meantime, mix together garlic powder, salt, dill, mustard, mayonnaise and yogurt in a small bowl.
- Transfer the cauliflower to an ungreased 3-cup baking dish, then put cheese and yogurt mixture on top. Bake at 350 degrees without a cover until cheese has melted and mixture is heated through, about 5 minutes.

Nutrition Information

- Calories: 88 calories
- Sodium: 222mg sodium
- Fiber: 2g fiber)
- Total Carbohydrate: 4g carbohydrate (2g sugars
- Cholesterol: 12mg cholesterol
- Protein: 4g protein. Diabetic Exchanges: 1-1/2 fat

- Total Fat: 7g fat (3g saturated fat)

169. Spiced Apple Gingerbread

Serving: 9 servings. | Prep: 15mins | Ready in:

Ingredients

- 2/3 cup sugar
- 1/3 cup unsweetened applesauce
- 1 egg
- 3 tablespoons molasses
- 1 cup all-purpose flour
- 1/2 cup whole wheat flour
- 2 teaspoons ground ginger
- 1 teaspoon baking powder
- 1 teaspoon baking soda
- 1 teaspoon ground cinnamon
- 1/4 teaspoon ground nutmeg
- 1/8 teaspoon ground allspice
- 1/2 cup reduced-fat plain yogurt
- 1-1/2 cups chopped peeled tart apple (about 1 medium)
- 1 cup plus 2 tablespoons reduced-fat whipped topping

Direction

- Mix together molasses, egg, applesauce and sugar in a big bowl. Mix together spices, baking soda, baking powder, ginger and flours, then put into the molasses mixture alternating with yogurt, while beating until just blended. Fold in the apples.
- Transfer into an 8-inch square baking dish sprayed with cooking spray. Bake at 350 degrees until a toothpick pricked in the center exits clean, about 30 to 35 minutes. Allow to cool on a wire rack, then slice into squares and dollop with whipped.

Nutrition Information

- Calories: 203 calories
- Protein: 4g protein.
- Total Fat: 2g fat (1g saturated fat)
- Sodium: 186mg sodium
- Fiber: 2g fiber)
- Total Carbohydrate: 42g carbohydrate (0 sugars
- Cholesterol: 24mg cholesterol

170. Spiced Cabbage And Apple Medley

Serving: 6 servings. | Prep: 20mins | Ready in:

Ingredients

- 1 medium head red cabbage, shredded
- 1 medium apple, peeled and thinly sliced
- 2/3 cup sugar
- 3/4 teaspoon salt
- 1/2 teaspoon dried rosemary, crushed
- 1/8 teaspoon pepper
- 2 bay leaves
- 4 whole cloves
- 1/3 cup cider vinegar
- 2 tablespoons lemon juice

Direction

- In a 6-quart stockpot, put apple and cabbage; toss in pepper, sugar, rosemary, and salt to combine. Set aside for 40 minutes to let the cabbage release the juices.
- In a double-thick cheesecloth, put cloves and bay leaves; collect the corners together to enclose the seasonings then secure with a string. Mix into the cabbage mixture.
- Boil on medium heat. Lower heat; let it simmer for 30-35 minutes while mixing from time to time, with cover, until the cabbage is tender. Mix in lemon juice and vinegar; heat completely. Remove the spice bag.

Nutrition Information

- Calories: 145 calories
- Protein: 2g protein.
- Total Fat: 0 fat (0 saturated fat)
- Sodium: 334mg sodium
- Fiber: 3g fiber)
- Total Carbohydrate: 36g carbohydrate (30g sugars
- Cholesterol: 0 cholesterol

171. Spiced Red Cabbage

Serving: Serves 8 | Prep: | Ready in:

Ingredients

- 1 medium head red cabbage (about 2 1/2 pounds)
- 2 tablespoons vegetable oil
- 3 tablespoons sugar
- 1 cup dry red wine
- 1/4 cup red-wine vinegar
- 1 bay leaf
- a 4-inch cinnamon stick
- 2 whole cloves

Direction

- Cut cabbage into quarters and core, then cut into shreds of 1/4-inch thickness. Cook cabbage in oil in a 7- to 8- quart heavy kettle over moderate heat for 5 minutes, stirring sometimes. Mix in the remaining ingredients; cover and simmer for about 20 minutes, stirring occasionally, until cabbage is soft. Pick out cloves and, if desired, cinnamon stick and bay leaf. Season cabbage with pepper and salt. Cabbage can be cooked 3 days in advance, covered and chilled.

Nutrition Information

- Calories: 111
- Total Carbohydrate: 16 g(5%)
- Protein: 2 g(4%)

- Total Fat: 4 g(6%)
- Saturated Fat: 0 g(1%)
- Sodium: 40 mg(2%)
- Fiber: 3 g(13%)

172. Spicy Brussels Sprouts And Carrots

Serving: 2 servings. | Prep: 10mins | Ready in:

Ingredients

- 3/4 cup fresh or frozen brussels sprouts, thawed and halved
- 3/4 cup sliced carrot
- 1/2 cup water
- 1/4 cup mayonnaise
- 2 teaspoons prepared horseradish
- 1 tablespoon finely chopped onion
- 1/8 teaspoon salt
- Dash pepper
- 1/4 cup soft bread crumbs
- 1-1/2 teaspoons butter, melted
- Minced fresh parsley

Direction

- Mix the initial 3 ingredients together in a small saucepan then lead the mixture to boiling point. Leave it cooking for 6 to 7 minutes with a cover on until the contents become tender and crispy before draining. Keep a tablespoon of the cooking liquid. Mix this reserved cooking liquid with pepper, salt, onion, horseradish and mayonnaise together in a bowl until combined. Insert the carrot and sprouts, tossing until coated. Move them into a 2-cup baking dish that has been greased. Mix butter and breadcrumbs together, sprinkling this over the top. Without any cover on, bake at 350°F until they turn a little brown or for 11 to 13 minutes. Scatter parsley over the top.

Nutrition Information

- Calories: 100 calories
- Total Fat: 4g fat (2g saturated fat)
- Sodium: 486mg sodium
- Fiber: 4g fiber)
- Total Carbohydrate: 15g carbohydrate (0 sugars
- Cholesterol: 11mg cholesterol
- Protein: 2g protein. Diabetic Exchanges: 1 starch

173. Spinach Slaw

Serving: 12-16 servings. | Prep: 20mins | Ready in:

Ingredients

- 8 cups shredded iceberg lettuce
- 5 cups shredded spinach
- 4 cups shredded red cabbage
- 3 cups shredded green cabbage
- 1 cup mayonnaise
- 1/4 cup honey
- 3/4 to 1 teaspoon garlic powder
- 1/2 teaspoon salt
- 1/4 teaspoon pepper

Direction

- Mix cabbage, spinach and lettuce in a large bowl; seal and allow to chill. Stir the remaining ingredients in a small bowl; seal and chill. Sprinkle dressing over the salad and mix to coat just before you serve.

Nutrition Information

- Calories: 132 calories
- Total Carbohydrate: 8g carbohydrate (6g sugars
- Cholesterol: 5mg cholesterol
- Protein: 1g protein.
- Total Fat: 11g fat (2g saturated fat)
- Sodium: 163mg sodium
- Fiber: 1g fiber)

- Sodium: 152mg sodium
- Fiber: 3g fiber)

174. Sprouts With Sour Cream

Serving: 12 servings. | Prep: 5mins | Ready in:

Ingredients

- 2 pounds fresh brussels sprouts, halved
- 1/2 cup chopped onion
- 2 tablespoons butter
- 1 tablespoon all-purpose flour
- 1 tablespoon brown sugar
- 1/2 teaspoon salt
- 1/2 teaspoon ground mustard
- 1/2 cup milk
- 1 cup (8 ounces) sour cream
- Minced fresh parsley

Direction

- In a saucepan, add 1 in. of water and Brussels sprouts then bring to a boil. Lower heat and cover the saucepan to simmer until tender for another 8-10 minutes.
- While vegetables are boiling, prepare another saucepan and sauté the onion in butter until softened. Stir in brown sugar, flour, mustard and salt until blended. Stir in milk gradually and bring the mixture up to a boil and continuously boil for 1 minute. Lower the heat and stir in the sour cream just until the mixture is warmed through.
- Drain the Brussels sprouts and transfer to a serving bowl. To finish, top with the sauce and a sprinkle of chopped parsley.

Nutrition Information

- Calories: 103 calories
- Total Carbohydrate: 10g carbohydrate (4g sugars
- Cholesterol: 19mg cholesterol
- Protein: 4g protein.
- Total Fat: 6g fat (4g saturated fat)

175. Steamed Winter Vegetables

Serving: 6 servings. | Prep: 15mins | Ready in:

Ingredients

- 1 pound small red potatoes, cut into 1-inch chunks
- 1/2 pound brussels sprouts, halved
- 2 medium parsnips, peeled and cut into 1/2-inch chunks
- 1 small turnip, peeled and cut into 1/2-inch chunks
- 2 small carrots, cut into 1/4- to 1/2-inch slices
- 4-1/2 teaspoons butter
- 1-1/2 teaspoons snipped fresh dill
- 1-1/2 teaspoons white vinegar
- 1-1/2 teaspoons prepared horseradish, drained
- 1/4 teaspoon salt

Direction

- Set the streamer basket over a big pot with an inch of boiling water; arrange vegetables in the basket then cover. Let it steam for 10-12mins until tender-crisp.
- In a big non-stick pan, melt butter; toss in vegetables until evenly coated. Mix salt, dill, horseradish, and vinegar in a small bowl; drizzle over the veggies. Mix to evenly coat. Serve right away.

Nutrition Information

- Calories: 123 calories
- Protein: 3g protein. Diabetic Exchanges: 1 starch
- Total Fat: 3g fat (2g saturated fat)
- Sodium: 162mg sodium

- Fiber: 4g fiber)
- Total Carbohydrate: 22g carbohydrate (0 sugars
- Cholesterol: 8mg cholesterol

176. Stewed Tomatoes With Dumplings

Serving: 2 servings. | Prep: 10mins | Ready in:

Ingredients

- 1 can (14-1/2 ounces) diced tomatoes, undrained
- 1 tablespoon sugar
- 1/4 teaspoon salt
- 1/4 teaspoon pepper
- 2 tablespoons butter
- 1/2 cup biscuit/baking mix
- 3 tablespoons milk

Direction

- Mix together butter, pepper, salt, sugar and tomatoes in a big saucepan. Bring to a boil on moderate heat while stirring sometimes.
- Mix milk and biscuit mix together in a small bowl. Drop batter into tomatoes in 4 mounds. Lower heat and simmer, covered, until a toothpick slid into a dumpling exits clean, about 10 minutes. Avoid lifting the cover while simmering.

Nutrition Information

- Calories: 302 calories
- Fiber: 4g fiber)
- Total Carbohydrate: 36g carbohydrate (14g sugars
- Cholesterol: 34mg cholesterol
- Protein: 5g protein.
- Total Fat: 17g fat (9g saturated fat)
- Sodium: 1061mg sodium

177. Stollen For A Crowd

Serving: 2 loaves (16 slices each). | Prep: 30mins | Ready in:

Ingredients

- 4-1/2 to 5-1/2 cups all-purpose flour
- 1 package (9 ounces) yellow cake mix
- 2 packages (1/4 ounce each) active dry yeast
- 1/4 teaspoon salt
- 2-1/2 cups warm water (120° to 130°)
- 2 cans (12-1/2 ounces each) poppy seed cake and pastry filling
- 1 tablespoon confectioners' sugar

Direction

- Mix together salt, yeast, cake mix and 3 cups of flour in a big bowl. Put into flour mixture with water and beat just until blended. Stir in enough quantity of flour to make a soft dough and the dough will be sticky.
- On a surface coated lightly with flour, turn dough out and knead for 6 to 8 minutes, until elastic and smooth. Put in a big bowl coated with grease and turn one time to grease top. Place a cover and allow to rise in a warm area for an hour, until doubled.
- Punch dough down and turn out on a surface coated with flour. Split the dough in 2 equal portions, then roll each into an oval, 12x8-inch in size. Use 1 can of filling to spread on each oval. Fold over with a long side to within 1 inch of opposite side, then seal by pressing edges slightly. Arrange on baking sheets coated with grease, then cover and allow to rise for a half hour, until doubled.
- Bake at 350 degrees until turn golden brown, about 25 to 30 minutes. Transfer to wire racks to cool, then use confectioners' sugar to sprinkle over top.

Nutrition Information

- Calories: 171 calories
- Cholesterol: 0 cholesterol
- Protein: 3g protein. Diabetic Exchanges: 2 starch
- Total Fat: 3g fat (1g saturated fat)
- Sodium: 87mg sodium
- Fiber: 1g fiber)
- Total Carbohydrate: 33g carbohydrate (4g sugars

178. Streusel Coffee Cake

Serving: 12 | Prep: | Ready in:

Ingredients

- 1 cup butter
- 2 cups white sugar
- 4 eggs
- 2 cups sour cream
- 2 teaspoons vanilla extract
- 4 cups all-purpose flour
- 2 teaspoons baking powder
- 2 teaspoons baking soda
- 1/2 cup white sugar
- 2 teaspoons ground cinnamon
- 1 cup chopped walnuts

Direction

- Preheat an oven to 175°C/350°F. Grease then flour the 10-in. Bundt pan. Mix baking soda, flour and baking powder in a medium bowl; put aside. Mix nuts, cinnamon and 1/2 cup sugar in another small bowl; put aside.
- Cream 2 cups white sugar and butter till fluffy and light in a big bowl. Add vanilla extract, sour cream and eggs. Add flour mixture; beat till combined well.
- Into Bundt pan, put 1/2 batter; sprinkle 1/2 nut mixture over batter in the pan. Add leftover batter; sprinkle final bits of nut mixture.
- Bake for 45-60 minutes at 175°C/350°F till an inserted toothpick in cake exits clean.

Nutrition Information

- Calories: 622 calories;
- Total Fat: 31.8
- Sodium: 445
- Total Carbohydrate: 77.2
- Cholesterol: 120
- Protein: 9.3

179. Strudel Sticks

Serving: 2 pastries (10 serving each). | Prep: 30mins | Ready in:

Ingredients

- 1 cup cold butter, cubed
- 2 cups all-purpose flour
- 1/2 cup sour cream
- 1 egg, separated
- 1 cup peach or apricot preserves, divided
- 30 vanilla wafers, crushed
- 1/2 cup sweetened shredded coconut
- 20 pecan halves
- GLAZE:
- 1/2 cup confectioners' sugar
- 1/8 teaspoon vanilla extract
- 2 to 3 teaspoons 2% milk

Direction

- Cut butter into flour until mixture forms coarse crumbs in a large bowl. Mix egg yolk and sour cream; then mix to flour mixture, use a fork to stir to make a soft dough. Split in half; use a plastic wrap to wrap. Place in the refrigerator for several hours or overnight. Roll each piece of dough into a 12 in. square on a floured surface. Scatter with preserves. Mix coconut and crushed wafers; drizzle over preserves. Turn up jolly - roll style; Secure the seam. On a baking sheet that is greased, place seam side down. Use a sharp knife to cut widthwise 3/4 of the way through that dough every 1 inch. Whisk egg whites until foamy; then brush on top of pastry. Put a pecan half on each slice. Place inside the oven and bake for 25 to 30 minutes at 350°F or until golden brown in color. Mix together the vanilla, enough milk and confectioners' sugar to reach the consistency that you want; sprinkle on top of pastries.

Nutrition Information

- Calories: 241 calories
- Fiber: 1g fiber)
- Total Carbohydrate: 29g carbohydrate (16g sugars
- Cholesterol: 40mg cholesterol
- Protein: 2g protein.
- Total Fat: 13g fat (7g saturated fat)
- Sodium: 124mg sodium

180. Stuffed Potato Dumplings

Serving: 15 dumplings. | Prep: 30mins | Ready in:

Ingredients

- CROUTONS:
- 1/4 cup butter
- 3 slices dry bread, cut into small cubes
- DUMPLINGS:
- 4 medium potatoes, peeled and quartered
- 1 cup all-purpose flour
- 1 teaspoon baking powder
- 1 teaspoon salt
- 2 teaspoons ground nutmeg
- 2 eggs, lightly beaten
- 2 teaspoons butter
- 2 tablespoons dry bread crumbs

Direction

- To make croutons, put butter in a small skillet, melt it; brown bread cubes. Set aside.
- Put potatoes covered in water in a saucepan then boil till potatoes become soft. Let it cool down; rice potatoes and transfer to a large bowl. Put in nutmeg, salt baking powder and flour. Put in eggs then stir; beat the mixture till it can hold its shape.
- Lightly flour your hands then form around 2 tablespoons dough into a ball, add some croutons in center of each ball. Keep making balls with crouton in the center with the rest of the croutons and dough. Keep in the fridge for an hour.
- Drop dumplings into boiling salted water (the ratio is 2 teaspoons salt for each quart of water). Let it simmer without a lid for 10 minutes. Drain. Put butter in a small skillet then melt butter; cook and stir the bread crumbs till it gets light brown color. Sprinkle on top of dumplings.

Nutrition Information

- Calories:
- Total Fat:
- Sodium:
- Fiber:
- Total Carbohydrate:
- Cholesterol:
- Protein:

181. Superb Herb Bread

Serving: 1 loaf (16 slices). | Prep: 10mins | Ready in:

Ingredients

- 1 cup warm fat-free milk (70° to 80°)
- 1 egg
- 2 tablespoons butter, softened, divided
- 2 tablespoons sugar
- 1 teaspoon salt
- 2 teaspoons caraway seeds
- 1-1/2 teaspoons poppy seeds
- 1-1/2 teaspoons dried minced onion

- 1 teaspoon rubbed sage
- 1/2 teaspoon ground nutmeg
- 2 cups bread flour
- 1 cup whole wheat flour
- 1-1/2 teaspoons active dry yeast

Direction

- Put milk, egg, 1 tablespoon of butter, sugar, salt, caraway seeds, poppy seeds, onion, sage, nutmeg, flours and yeast in the bread machine pan according to the order on the machine's manual. Use the dough setting (once five minutes of mixing elapse, check the dough and add one to two tablespoons of flour or water if necessary).
- Once the cycle is finished, turn the dough on a surface that is lightly floured. Then punch the dough down and form into a loaf. Transfer into a loaf pan of 9x5-in. that is greased with cooking spray. Cover the loaf and allow to rise for about 45 minutes until doubled.
- Bake for about 30 to 35 minutes at 350 degrees F or until turned golden brown. Transfer from the pan onto wire rack. Then melt the remaining butter and rub onto the loaf.

Nutrition Information

- Calories: 109 calories
- Sodium: 174mg sodium
- Fiber: 2g fiber)
- Total Carbohydrate: 19g carbohydrate (0 sugars
- Cholesterol: 17mg cholesterol
- Protein: 4g protein. Diabetic Exchanges: 1 starch
- Total Fat: 2g fat (1g saturated fat)

182. Sweet Sour Red Cabbage

Serving: 2 servings. | Prep: 10mins | Ready in:

Ingredients

- 2 tablespoons cider vinegar
- 1 tablespoon brown sugar
- 1/4 teaspoon caraway seeds
- 1/4 teaspoon celery seed
- 2 cups shredded red cabbage
- 1/2 cup thinly sliced onion
- Salt and pepper to taste

Direction

- Mix together celery seeds, caraway, brown sugar and vinegar in a small bowl, then put aside. Put in a saucepan with onion and cabbage, and then put in a little amount of water. Place a cover and steam for 15 minutes, until softened.
- Put in vinegar mixture and toss to coat well. Use pepper and salt to season, then serve warm.

Nutrition Information

- Calories: 60 calories
- Cholesterol: 0 cholesterol
- Protein: 1g protein.
- Total Fat: 0 fat (0 saturated fat)
- Sodium: 12mg sodium
- Fiber: 2g fiber)
- Total Carbohydrate: 15g carbohydrate (12g sugars

183. Sweet Sour Red Cabbage Side Dish

Serving: 8 servings. | Prep: 15mins | Ready in:

Ingredients

- 1 medium head red cabbage, shredded
- 1 large onion, chopped
- 1/4 cup canola oil
- 2 medium apples, peeled and thinly sliced
- 1/4 cup cider vinegar
- 1/2 teaspoon salt

- 1/4 teaspoon pepper
- 2 tablespoons maraschino cherry juice, optional

Direction

- In the big skillet, sauté the onion and cabbage in oil till tender-crisp or for 5 to 8 minutes. If you want, put in the cherry juice, pepper, salt, vinegar and apples. Boil. Lower the heat; keep covered and let simmer till the cabbage softens or for 25 minutes.

Nutrition Information

- Calories: 112 calories
- Protein: 2g protein. Diabetic Exchanges: 1 vegetable
- Total Fat: 7g fat (1g saturated fat)
- Sodium: 160mg sodium
- Fiber: 3g fiber)
- Total Carbohydrate: 13g carbohydrate (9g sugars
- Cholesterol: 0 cholesterol

184. Sweet And Sour Red Cabbage

Serving: Serves 8 | Prep: | Ready in:

Ingredients

- 3 tablespoons butter
- 1 red onion, halved, thinly sliced
- 1 3/4 teaspoons caraway seeds
- 1 2-pound head red cabbage, cored, thinly sliced (about 12 cups)
- 1/3 cup red wine vinegar
- 1/4 cup sugar
- 1/4 cup minced fresh dill

Direction

- In big pot, liquify butter on moderate heat. Put in caraway and onion. Place cover; let cook for 3 minutes. Put in cabbage. Place cover; cook for 6 minutes till cabbage starts to become tender, mixing from time to time. Put sugar and vinegar; cook till cabbage turn crisp-tender, mixing frequently, for an additional of 4 minutes. Put in dill. Add pepper and salt to season.

Nutrition Information

- Calories: 114
- Saturated Fat: 3 g(14%)
- Sodium: 38 mg(2%)
- Fiber: 3 g(13%)
- Total Carbohydrate: 18 g(6%)
- Cholesterol: 11 mg(4%)
- Protein: 2 g(4%)
- Total Fat: 5 g(7%)

185. Three Flour Braid

Serving: 2 loaves (16 slices each). | Prep: 40mins | Ready in:

Ingredients

- 2 packages (1/4 ounce each) active dry yeast
- 2-1/4 cups warm water (110° to 115°)
- 1/4 cup canola oil
- 2 tablespoons sugar
- 1 teaspoon salt
- 3-1/4 cups all-purpose flour
- RYE DOUGH:
- 2 tablespoons molasses
- 1 tablespoon baking cocoa
- 1 teaspoon caraway seeds
- 1-1/4 cups rye flour
- WHEAT DOUGH:
- 2 tablespoons molasses
- 1 cup whole wheat flour
- WHITE DOUGH:
- 1-1/4 cups all-purpose flour
- 1 tablespoon butter, melted

Direction

- Dissolve yeast in a big bowl with water. Put in 2 1/4 cups of all-purpose flour, salt, sugar and oil, then beat the mixture about 2 minutes. Put in leftover all-purpose flour, then beat about 2 minutes more. Split the mixture evenly into 3 bowls.
- With the 1st bowl, put in caraway, cocoa and molasses, mixing well. Put in rye flour slowly. Turn the dough out on a surface coated with flour and knead for 6 to 8 minutes, until elastic and smooth. Put in a bowl coated with grease and turn one time to grease top. Place a cover and put aside.
- With the 2nd bowl, put in molasses and blend well. Put in whole wheat flour gradually. Turn dough out on a surface coated with flour and knead for 6 to 8 minutes, until elastic and smooth. Put in a bowl coated with grease and turn one time to grease top. Place a cover and put aside.
- With the 3rd bowl, put in all-purpose flour gradually. Turn the dough out on a surface coated with flour and knead for 6 to 8 minutes, until elastic and smooth. Put in a bowl coated with grease and turn one time to grease top. Cover entire of 3 bowls and allow to rise in a warm area for an hour, until doubled.
- Punch doughs down. Turn out on a surface coated lightly with flour, then split each in 2 even portions. Form each half into a 15-inch rope. Put on a baking sheet coated with grease with a rope of each dough and braid, then seal by pinching ends and tuck beneath. Do the same process with leftover ropes. Cover and allow to rise for a half hour, until almost doubled.
- Bake for 25 to 30 minutes at 350 degrees, until turn golden brown. Use butter to brush the surface then transfer from pan to a wire rack to cool.

Nutrition Information

- Calories: 120 calories
- Total Fat: 2g fat (0 saturated fat)
- Sodium: 79mg sodium
- Fiber: 2g fiber)
- Total Carbohydrate: 22g carbohydrate (3g sugars
- Cholesterol: 1mg cholesterol
- Protein: 3g protein.

186. Toasted Muesli

Serving: 7 servings. | Prep: 10mins | Ready in:

Ingredients

- 2 cups old-fashioned oats
- 1/4 cup sunflower kernels
- 1/4 cup sliced almonds
- 1/3 cup finely chopped dates
- 2 tablespoons oat bran
- 1 cup bran flakes
- 1/4 cup toasted wheat germ
- 1/4 cup raisins
- 1 tablespoon sugar
- 1-3/4 cups fat-free milk, optional

Direction

- Mix almonds, sunflower kernels and oats in a 15x10x1-inch baking pan. Bake till almonds are golden for 10-15 minutes at 350°.
- Put oat bran and dates in a big bowl; mix to coat dates in oat bran. Add sugar, raisins, wheat germ, bran flakes and oat mixture; gently mix to combine. If desired, serve with milk. Keep in an airtight container.

Nutrition Information

- Calories: 217 calories
- Sodium: 13mg sodium
- Fiber: 5g fiber)
- Total Carbohydrate: 35g carbohydrate (0 sugars
- Cholesterol: 0 cholesterol

- Protein: 8g protein. Diabetic Exchanges: 2 starch
- Total Fat: 7g fat (1g saturated fat)

187. Toasted Veggie Sandwich

Serving: 1 serving. | Prep: 10mins | Ready in:

Ingredients

- 1 teaspoon fat-free mayonnaise
- 1 teaspoon spicy brown or horseradish mustard
- 2 slices rye bread
- 1 slice (1 ounce) reduced-fat Swiss cheese, cut in half
- 3 tablespoons grated carrot
- 1 tablespoon finely chopped onion
- 2 tablespoons sauerkraut, well drained and chopped
- 1/2 cup thinly sliced fresh spinach
- Refrigerated butter-flavored spray

Direction

- On each slice of bread, spread the mustard and mayonnaise. Layer a half slice of cheese, carrot, onions sauerkraut spinach and leftover cheese on one piece of bread, then cover with the 2nd piece of bread. Use chilled butter-flavored spray to spray both sides of the sandwich. Toast the sandwich in a small nonstick frying pan on medium heat, until the bread browns on both sides.

Nutrition Information

- Calories: 290 calories
- Sodium: 727mg sodium
- Fiber: 5g fiber)
- Total Carbohydrate: 37g carbohydrate (0 sugars
- Cholesterol: 19mg cholesterol
- Protein: 15g protein. Diabetic Exchanges: 2 starch
- Total Fat: 9g fat (5g saturated fat)

188. Traditional Stollen

Serving: 2 loaves. | Prep: 30mins | Ready in:

Ingredients

- 1 package (1/4 ounce) active dry yeast
- 2 tablespoons warm water (110° to 115°)
- 1 cup warm 2% milk (110° to 115°)
- 3/4 cup butter, softened
- 1/2 cup sugar
- 2 large eggs, lightly beaten
- 1-1/2 teaspoons grated lemon zest
- 1/2 teaspoon salt
- 4-3/4 to 5-1/4 cups all-purpose flour
- 3/4 cup raisins
- 1/2 cup mixed candied fruit
- 1/2 cup chopped almonds
- GLAZE:
- 1-1/2 cups confectioners' sugar
- 2 to 3 tablespoons 2% milk

Direction

- Melt yeast in warm water in a big bowl. Add 3 cups flour, lemon zest, eggs, sugar, butter, milk; add almonds, candied fruit and raisins; add enough leftover flour to make soft dough.
- Turn on the floured surface; knead for roughly 6-8 minutes till elastic and smooth. Put in the greased bowl; turn it once to grease the top. Cover; rise for 1 1/2 hours in a warm place till doubled.
- Punch down dough; halve. Cover; rest for 10 minutes. Press/roll each half to a 12x7-in. oval. Within 1-in. of opposite edges, fold the long side over; lightly press edge to seal. Put on the greased baking sheets; slightly curve ends. Cover; rise for about 1 hour till nearly doubled.

- Bake till golden brown for 25-30 minutes at 375°; on wire racks, cool. Mix confectioners' sugar and enough milk to get preferred consistency; spread on stollen.

Nutrition Information

- Calories: 244 calories
- Total Fat: 8g fat (4g saturated fat)
- Sodium: 75mg sodium
- Fiber: 2g fiber)
- Total Carbohydrate: 40g carbohydrate (18g sugars
- Cholesterol: 35mg cholesterol
- Protein: 4g protein.

189. Tricolor Braid

Serving: 2 loaves (12 slices each). | Prep: 60mins | Ready in:

Ingredients

- 2 packages (1/4 ounce each) active dry yeast
- 2-1/3 cups warm water (110° to 115°)
- 1/4 cup butter, softened
- 2 tablespoons honey
- 3 teaspoons salt
- 3-1/3 to 3-2/3 cups all-purpose flour
- WHEAT DOUGH:
- 2 tablespoons toasted wheat germ
- 2 tablespoons molasses
- 1 cup plus 2 to 5 tablespoons whole wheat flour
- PUMPERNICKEL DOUGH:
- 2 tablespoons baking cocoa
- 2 tablespoons molasses
- 1 cup plus 2 to 5 tablespoons rye flour
- 1 egg white
- 1 tablespoon water

Direction

- Dissolve yeast in a big bowl with warm water, then put in 2 1/3 cups of flour, salt, honey and butter. Beat the mixture about 2 minutes, then split between 3 bowls evenly.
- To the 1st bowl, stir in enough amount of leftover all-purpose flour to make a stiff dough.
- Turn dough out on a surface coated with flour and knead about 6 to 8 minutes, until elastic and smooth. Put dough into a bowl coated with grease and turn one time to coat top. Place a cover and put aside.
- Put into the 2nd bowl with molasses and wheat germ, beating until smooth. Stir in enough amount of wheat flour to form a stiff dough.
- Turn dough out on a surface coated with flour and knead for 6 to 8 minutes, until elastic and smooth. Put dough into a bowl greased with cooking spray and turn one time to grease top. Place a cover and put aside.
- To the 3rd bowl, put in molasses and cocoa, beating until smooth. Stir in enough amount of rye flour to form a stiff dough.
- Turn dough out on a surface coated with flour and knead for 6 to 8 minutes, until elastic and smooth. Put dough into a bowl coated with grease and turn one time to coat top. Place a cover and allow entire of 3 bowls to rise in a warm area for an hour, until doubled.
- Punch doughs down then split each dough in 2 even portions. Form each portion into a 15-inch rope. Position a rope of each dough on a baking sheet coated with grease and braid, then seal ends. Do the same process with leftover ropes.
- Cover and allow to rise for 45 minutes, until doubled. Beat water and egg white together, then brush over braids.
- Bake about 25 to 30 minutes at 350 degrees, until turn golden brown. Transfer to wire racks to cool.

Nutrition Information

- Calories: 146 calories

- Protein: 4g protein. Diabetic Exchanges: 2 starch
- Total Fat: 2g fat (1g saturated fat)
- Sodium: 319mg sodium
- Fiber: 2g fiber)
- Total Carbohydrate: 28g carbohydrate (4g sugars
- Cholesterol: 5mg cholesterol

190. Triple Mushroom Stroganoff

Serving: 6 servings. | Prep: 20mins | Ready in:

Ingredients

- 5-1/2 cups uncooked egg noodles
- 1/2 pound fresh button mushrooms, halved
- 2-2/3 cups sliced baby portobello mushrooms
- 1 package (3-1/2 ounces) sliced fresh shiitake mushrooms
- 3 shallots, chopped
- 2 tablespoons butter
- 3 garlic cloves, minced
- 1-1/2 cups vegetable broth, divided
- 2 teaspoons Dijon mustard
- 1/2 teaspoon salt
- 1/4 teaspoon pepper
- 2 tablespoons all-purpose flour
- 1 cup (8 ounces) fat-free sour cream
- 1 tablespoon minced fresh parsley

Direction

- Following package directions to cook noodles. In the meantime, cook shallots and mushrooms in a big nonstick skillet with butter on moderate heat until soft, about 6 to 8 minutes. Put in garlic and cook for 1 more minute.
- Stir in pepper, salt, mustard and 1 1/4 cups of broth, then bring mixture to a boil. Lower heat and simmer without a cover about 10 minutes while stirring sometimes.
- Mix leftover broth and flour together until smooth, then stir into mushroom mixture gradually. Bring to a boil then cook and stir until bubbly and thickened, about 2 minutes. Lower heat to low and stir in sour cream gradually without boiling. Drain noodles and serve together with mushroom sauce. Sprinkle parsley over top.

Nutrition Information

- Calories: 296 calories
- Protein: 12g protein.
- Total Fat: 6g fat (3g saturated fat)
- Sodium: 575mg sodium
- Fiber: 2g fiber)
- Total Carbohydrate: 49g carbohydrate (6g sugars
- Cholesterol: 57mg cholesterol

191. Two Cabbage Slaw

Serving: Serves 2 to 3 | Prep: | Ready in:

Ingredients

- 1 carrot, shredded fine
- 1 1/2 cups thinly sliced green cabbage (about 1/4 head)
- 1 1/2 cups thinly sliced red cabbage (about 1/4 head)
- 1 1/2 tablespoons extra-virgin olive oil
- 2 teaspoons rice vinegar (not seasoned)
- 1/2 teaspoon sugar

Direction

- Toss the cabbages and the carrot together in a bowl and drizzle it with oil. To coat, toss it. Put in the pepper, salt, sugar and vinegar to taste. Toss well. Let it stand for 10 minutes.

Nutrition Information

- Calories: 169
- Total Fat: 10 g(16%)
- Saturated Fat: 1 g(7%)
- Sodium: 71 mg(3%)
- Fiber: 6 g(24%)
- Total Carbohydrate: 19 g(6%)
- Protein: 3 g(7%)

192. Vegetable Stuffing Bake

Serving: 2 casseroles (6-8 servings each). | Prep: 20mins | Ready in:

Ingredients

- 1 medium onion, chopped
- 1 tablespoon canola oil
- 2 cans (10-3/4 ounces each) condensed cream of mushroom soup, undiluted
- 1 cup process cheese sauce
- 1 package (16 ounces) frozen cauliflower, thawed
- 1 package (16 ounces) frozen corn, thawed
- 1 package (16 ounces) frozen broccoli florets, thawed
- 1 package (16 ounces) frozen brussels sprouts, thawed and halved
- 1 package (6 ounces) corn bread stuffing mix, divided

Direction

- Sauté onion with oil in a big skillet until it is tender. Add the cheese sauce and soup, stir until blended; heat well. Mix 1 cup of stuffing mix and the vegetables in a big bowl. Mix in soup mixture and combine.
- Place in two shallow 2-qt. baking dishes that are greased. Spread the leftover stuffing mix. Uncover and bake at 350 until vegetables become tender and bubbles appears in the edges, or for 30 to 35 minutes.

Nutrition Information

- Calories: 120 calories
- Sodium: 345mg sodium
- Fiber: 4g fiber)
- Total Carbohydrate: 21g carbohydrate (4g sugars
- Cholesterol: 1mg cholesterol
- Protein: 5g protein.
- Total Fat: 3g fat (0 saturated fat)

193. Vegetarian Reubens

Serving: 6 | Prep: 10mins | Ready in:

Ingredients

- 1 pound smoked Cheddar cheese, shredded
- 1 cup thousand island salad dressing, or to taste
- 1 (16 ounce) jar sauerkraut, drained
- 12 slices dark rye bread
- 2 tablespoons butter
- 2 tomatoes, sliced

Direction

- Mix together the sauerkraut and cheese in a big mixing bowl, then add enough dressing to coat and stir thoroughly.
- Put butter on one side of each bread slice. On the unbuttered side of half of the slices of bread, spread a thick layer of the cheese mixture, then put sliced tomato and another bread slice on top.
- Heat a big frying pan to medium-high heat, then fry the sandwiches on both sides until the cheese melts and exterior becomes toasted.

Nutrition Information

- Calories: 710 calories;
- Total Carbohydrate: 46.6
- Cholesterol: 104
- Protein: 25.4
- Total Fat: 48.2

- Sodium: 1903

194. Veggie Turkey Centerpiece

Serving: 1 centerpiece. | Prep: 60mins | Ready in:

Ingredients

- 7 radishes
- 13 kale leaves, divided
- 1 medium head cabbage
- 1 medium carrot, peeled
- Toothpicks
- 2 raisins
- 2 pimiento strips (1-1/4 inches long)
- 1 small head red cabbage
- 12 cherry tomatoes
- 18 pimiento-stuffed olives
- 2 cans (6 ounces each) pitted ripe olives, drained

Direction

- With each radish, trim the 2 ends. Slice radishes using a sharp knife to shape into roses. Put into a bowl containing ice water; chill for half an hour until radishes open.
- Line 6 kale leaves onto a serving platter. Cut off the bottom of medium cabbage to make it level; put on the platter to make turkey body.
- Cut out a 1-1/2-inch piece and 3-1/2-inch piece from the carrot (Throw away the rest of the carrot or keep for later use). Create a diagonal cut at one end of each piece.
- To form a beak, create a V-shape cut at the second end of small carrot piece. Stick the diagonal end of the bigger carrot piece to the turkey body with toothpicks to create the neck.
- To make the head, stick the diagonal end of smaller carrot piece to the neck. To make eyes, attach raisins and to make wattle, attach pimiento strips, using toothpicks.
- To make the tail, pin the rest of kale leaves to the back. Take 8 leaves away from the red cabbage; attach to the front of kale leaves. (Keep the rest of cabbage for later use). Stick cherry tomatoes to the front of cabbage leaves.
- Attach stuffed olives to make wings. Use ripe olives to cover the rest of the body. Decorate the plate with roses made from radish.

Nutrition Information

- Calories:
- Sodium:
- Fiber:
- Total Carbohydrate:
- Cholesterol:
- Protein:
- Total Fat:

195. Waffled Soft Pretzels

Serving: 1 dozen. | Prep: 45mins | Ready in:

Ingredients

- 2 teaspoons active dry yeast
- 1-1/3 cups warm water (110° to 115°)
- 1/3 cup packed brown sugar
- 1/4 teaspoon kosher salt
- 3-1/2 to 4 cups bread flour
- 6 cups water
- 1/4 cup baking soda
- 2 tablespoons butter, melted
- Additional kosher salt

Direction

- Dissolve yeast in a big bowl filled with warm water. Put in 2 cups of flour, salt and brown sugar, then beat until the mixture is smooth. Stir in a sufficient amount of leftover flour to make a soft dough.
- Turn dough out on a surface coated with flour and knead for 4 to 6 minutes, or until you get

an elastic and smooth dough. Put dough into a bowl coated with grease, flipping one time to grease the top. Cover bowl and allow dough to rise in a warm area for 45 minutes, or until doubled.

- Punch dough down and split it into 12 pieces. Roll each pieces into a rope with size of 18 inches, then twist it into a pretzel shape. Allow to rest, covered, about 10 minutes.
- Bring baking soda and water in a big saucepan to a boil. Put into the boiling water with one pretzel at a time, about a half minute. Use a slotted spoon to take pretzel out of the water and transfer on paper towels to drain.
- On a preheated waffle iron sprayed with cooking spray, add pretzels, then cook until turn golden brown, about 1-1 1/2 minutes. Transfer to a wire racks carefully, then use butter to brush cooked pretzels instantly. Sprinkle more salt on top and serve warm.

Nutrition Information

- Calories:
- Cholesterol:
- Protein:
- Total Fat:
- Sodium:
- Fiber:
- Total Carbohydrate:

196. Walnut Filled Stollen

Serving: 3 loaves (5 slices each). | Prep: 30mins | Ready in:

Ingredients

- 1 package (1/4 ounce) active dry yeast
- 1 cup warm milk (110° to 115°)
- 1/2 cup butter, softened
- 1/2 cup sugar
- 2 eggs
- 1 teaspoon salt
- 4 to 4-1/2 cups all-purpose flour
- FILLING:
- 3 cups chopped walnuts
- 1 cup packed brown sugar
- 2 tablespoons half-and-half cream
- 1 tablespoon vanilla extract
- 2 teaspoons ground cinnamon
- Vanilla Drizzle

Direction

- Dissolve yeast in a big bowl with warm milk. Put in 2 cups of flour, salt, eggs, sugar and butter, beating well until smooth. Stir in enough amount of leftover flour to make a soft dough. Turn dough out on a surface coated with flour and knead for 6 to 8 minutes, until elastic and smooth. Put dough into a bowl coated with grease and turn one time to grease top. Place a cover and allow to rise in a warm area for 1 1/4 hours, until doubled.
- Punch dough down and split into 3 portions. Form each into an oval, 12x7-inch in size. Mix together cinnamon, vanilla, cream, brown sugar and walnuts in a bowl, then spread the mixture down the center third of each stollen. Fold over filling with a long side to within 1 inch of opposite side, then seal by pressing edge slightly. Put on baking sheets coated with grease then curve ends somewhat. Place a cover and allow to rise for 45 minutes, until almost doubled.
- Bake at 350 degrees until turn golden brown, about 15 to 20 minutes. Transfer to wire racks to cool. Put Vanilla Drizzle on top.

Nutrition Information

- Calories: 136 calories
- Cholesterol: 15mg cholesterol
- Protein: 4g protein.
- Total Fat: 7g fat (2g saturated fat)
- Sodium: 76mg sodium
- Fiber: 1g fiber)
- Total Carbohydrate: 16g carbohydrate (7g sugars

197. Wild Rice Bread

Serving: 1 loaf, 16 slices (1-1/2 pounds). | Prep: 10mins | Ready in:

Ingredients

- 3/4 cup water (70° to 80°)
- 1 tablespoon vegetable oil
- 1 tablespoon molasses
- 1 teaspoon salt
- 1-2/3 cups bread flour
- 1/2 cup cooked wild rice, cooked
- 1/2 cup whole wheat flour
- 1 teaspoon caraway seeds
- 1 teaspoon active dry yeast

Direction

- Put all the ingredients into the pan of bread machine in the order recommended by the manufacturer. Use the basic bread setting. If available, select the crust color and loaf size. Then bake as directed by the bread machine (after five minutes of mixing elapse, check the dough and you can add one to two tablespoons of flour or water if necessary).

Nutrition Information

- Calories: 82 calories
- Fiber: 0 fiber)
- Total Carbohydrate: 15g carbohydrate (0 sugars
- Cholesterol: 0 cholesterol
- Protein: 3g protein. Diabetic Exchanges: 1 starch.
- Total Fat: 1g fat (0 saturated fat)
- Sodium: 147mg sodium

198. Winter Root Vegetables

Serving: 10-12 servings. | Prep: 30mins | Ready in:

Ingredients

- 2 pounds small red potatoes, quartered
- 1 pound brussels sprouts, halved
- 1/2 pound parsnips, peeled and julienned
- 1/2 pound carrots, cut into chunks
- 1/2 pound turnips, peeled and cut into chunks
- 1/2 cup butter, cubed
- 2 tablespoons prepared horseradish
- 2 tablespoons cider vinegar
- 2 tablespoons snipped fresh dill or 2 teaspoons dill weed
- 1/2 teaspoon salt, optional
- 1/4 teaspoon pepper

Direction

- Separately cook the veggies in water until they are tender; drain. Mix the remaining ingredients with melted butter. Mix the butter mixture and the veggies together until evenly coated.

Nutrition Information

- Calories: 97 calories
- Total Fat: 5g fat (0 saturated fat)
- Sodium: 72mg sodium
- Fiber: 0 fiber)
- Total Carbohydrate: 12g carbohydrate (0 sugars
- Cholesterol: 0 cholesterol
- Protein: 2g protein. Diabetic Exchanges: 1 vegetable

199. Winter Vegetable Medley

Serving: 8 servings. | Prep: 15mins | Ready in:

Ingredients

- 1/2 pound fresh Brussels sprouts, halved
- 1/2 pound parsnips, peeled and cut into 1/2-inch cubes
- 1/2 pound fresh baby carrots

- 1 medium sweet potato, peeled and cut into 1/2-inch cubes
- 2 medium red potatoes, cut into 1/2-inch cubes
- 2 medium white potatoes, peeled and cut into 1/2-inch cubes
- 1/2 cup butter, melted
- 1-1/2 teaspoons rubbed sage
- 2 garlic cloves, minced

Direction

- On a 13-inch by 9-inch baking dish that has been greased, set the vegetables down. Mix garlic, sage and butter together in a small bowl then empty this mixture into the baking dish on the veggies. Leave it baking at 375°F with a cover on until the vegetables tenderize, about 40 to 50 minutes

Nutrition Information

- Calories: 0

200. Wisconsin Cheddar Cider Spread

Serving: 1-1/4 cups. | Prep: 10mins | Ready in:

Ingredients

- 1/2 cup apple cider or juice
- 2 tablespoons reduced-fat plain yogurt
- 1 tablespoon prepared mustard
- 2 cups shredded cheddar cheese
- 2 teaspoons caraway seeds
- Apple slices and/or rye crackers

Direction

- Mix together cheese, mustard, yogurt and apple cider in a blender, then cover and process until combined. Stir in caraway seeds, then cover and chill for a minimum of an hour. Serve together with crackers and/or apples.

Nutrition Information

- Calories: 90 calories
- Cholesterol: 24mg cholesterol
- Protein: 5g protein.
- Total Fat: 7g fat (5g saturated fat)
- Sodium: 156mg sodium
- Fiber: 0 fiber)
- Total Carbohydrate: 3g carbohydrate (2g sugars

201. Zesty Slaw

Serving: about 85 servings. | Prep: 25mins | Ready in:

Ingredients

- 8 quarts shredded cabbage
- 8 quarts shredded red cabbage
- 2-1/2 cups grated carrots
- 3 cups mayonnaise
- 1 cup sour cream
- 1/2 cup grated onion
- 1/2 cup chopped fresh parsley
- 1/2 cup cider vinegar
- 3 tablespoons Dijon mustard
- 2 tablespoons celery seed
- 2 teaspoons salt
- 2 teaspoons pepper

Direction

- Mix carrots and cabbage in several large bowls. Mix all the remaining ingredients until well blended. Pour it all over the cabbage mixture, tossing well to coat. Cover the bowl and refrigerate for several hours.

Nutrition Information

- Calories: 79 calories
- Protein: 1g protein.
- Total Fat: 7g fat (1g saturated fat)

- Sodium: 122mg sodium
- Fiber: 1g fiber)
- Total Carbohydrate: 4g carbohydrate (2g sugars
- Cholesterol: 5mg cholesterol

202. Zwieback Rolls

Serving: 2 dozen. | *Prep: 30mins* | *Ready in:*

Ingredients

- 1 package (1/4 ounce) active dry yeast
- 1/4 cup warm water (110° to 115°)
- 1-3/4 cups milk, scalded
- 1/2 cup shortening
- 1/4 cup sugar
- 2 teaspoons salt
- 5 to 6 cups all-purpose flour

Direction

- In warm water, dissolve yeast, then put aside. Mix together the shortening and milk in a big bowl, mixing to melt the shortening. Once cooled, add salt and sugar. Mix in 3 cups of flour and yeast mixture, then beat well. Add enough of the leftover flour until a soft dough forms. Flip out onto a surface covered with a thin layer of flour and knead for around 6 to 8 minutes until pliable and smooth. Put the dough in a bowl coated with cooking spray, flipping once to grease the top. Put on a cover and allow to rise for about an hour in a warm area until doubled. Punch the dough down and split into fourths. Split 3 of the pieces into 8 pieces each, then form into smooth balls and put on greased baking sheets. Split the 4th piece of the dough into 24 small balls. Create an indentation in the top of each bigger ball, then press 1 small ball over each bigger ball. Put on a cover and allow to rise for about 45 minutes in a warm area, until doubled. Bake for 20 to 25 minutes at 375 degrees or until golden brown.

Nutrition Information

- Calories: 142 calories
- Cholesterol: 1mg cholesterol
- Protein: 3g protein. Diabetic Exchanges: 1-1/2 starch
- Total Fat: 4g fat (0 saturated fat)
- Sodium: 201mg sodium
- Fiber: 0 fiber)
- Total Carbohydrate: 23g carbohydrate (0 sugars

Index

A

B

C

D

E

F

G

H

L

M

N

O

P

R

S

T

V

W

Y

Z

Conclusion

Thank you again for downloading this book!

I hope you enjoyed reading about my book!

If you enjoyed this book, please take the time to share your thoughts and post a review on Amazon. It'd be greatly appreciated!

Write me an honest review about the book – I truly value your opinion and thoughts and I will incorporate them into my next book, which is already underway.

Thank you!

If you have any questions, **feel free to contact at:** *author@basilrecipes.com*

Judy Davis

basilrecipes.com

Printed in Poland
by Amazon Fulfillment
Poland Sp. z o.o., Wrocław

85055694R00065